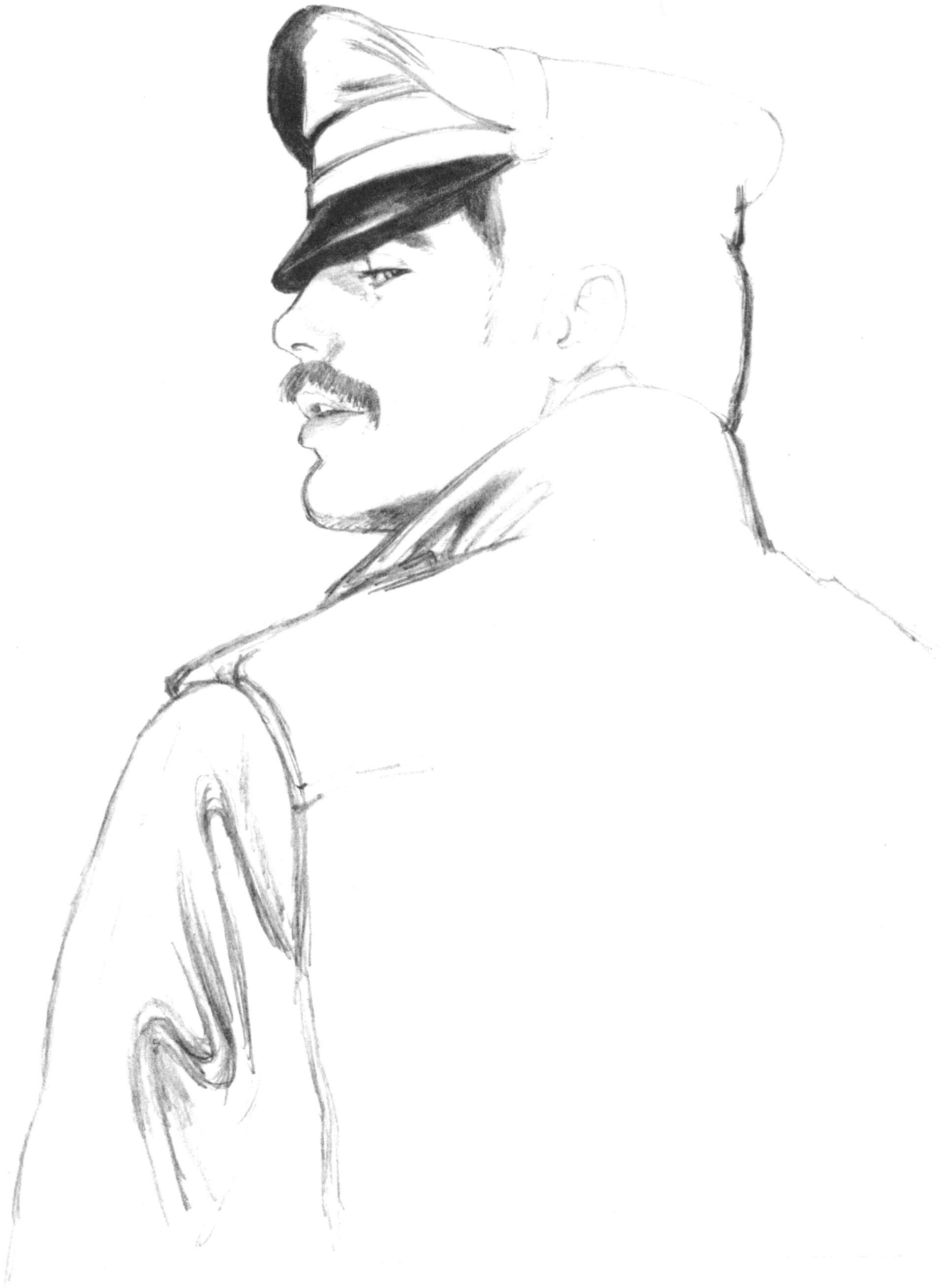

Tom of Finland

SKIRA

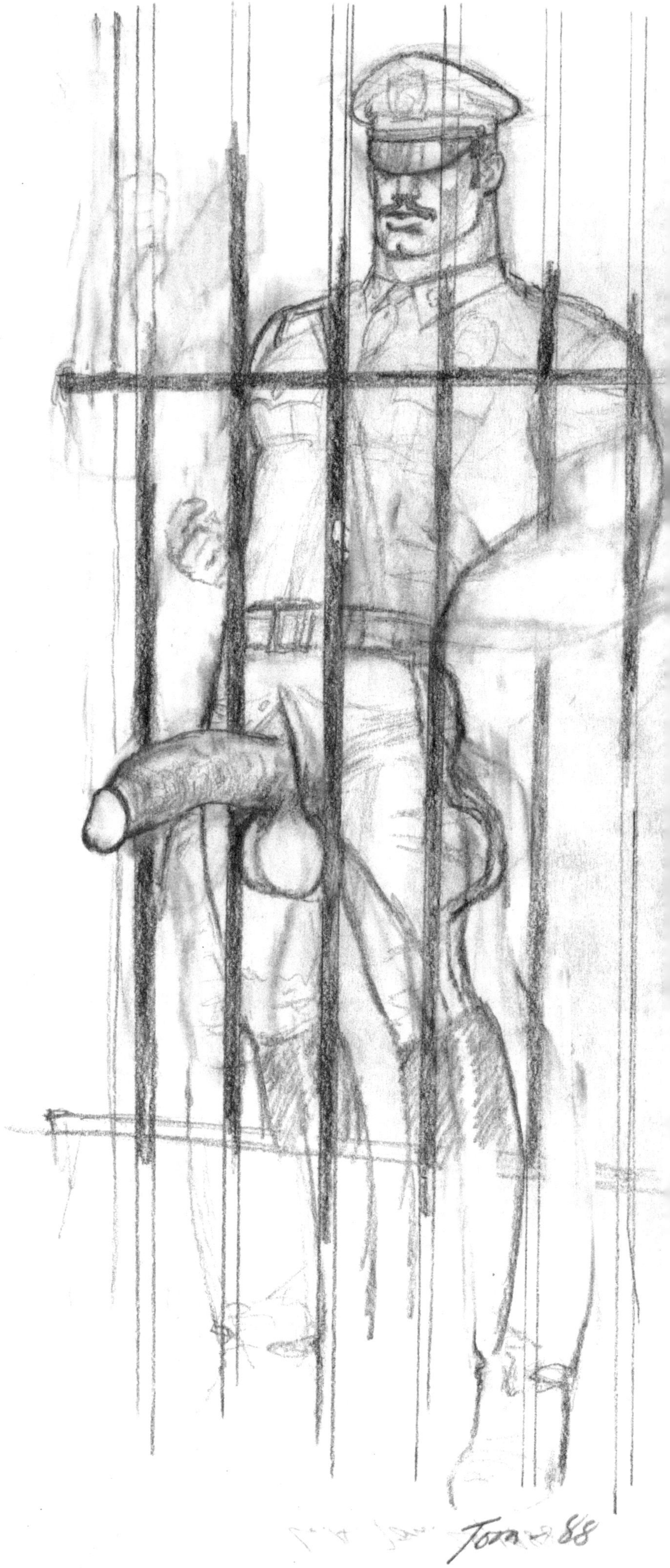
Tom 88

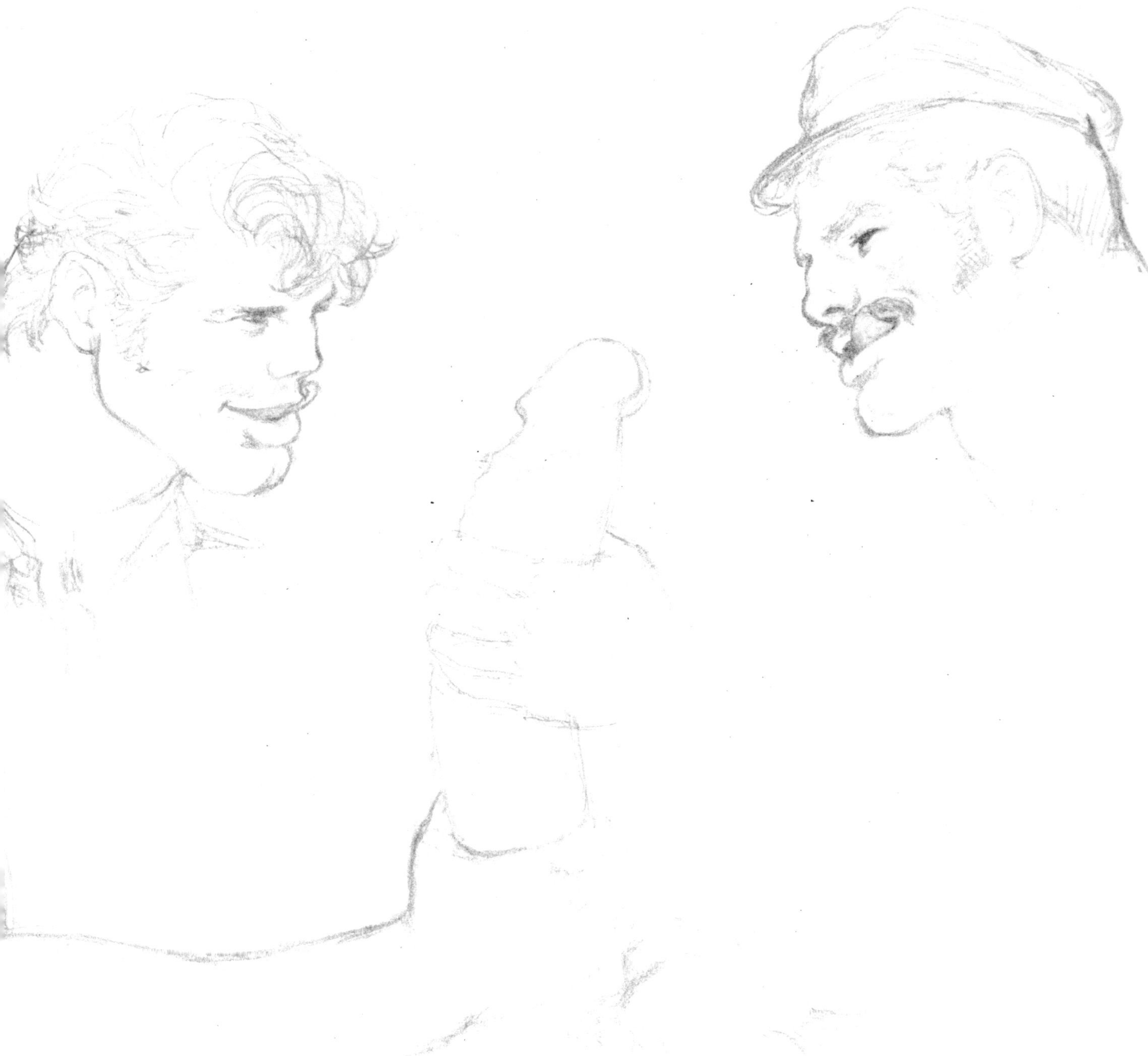

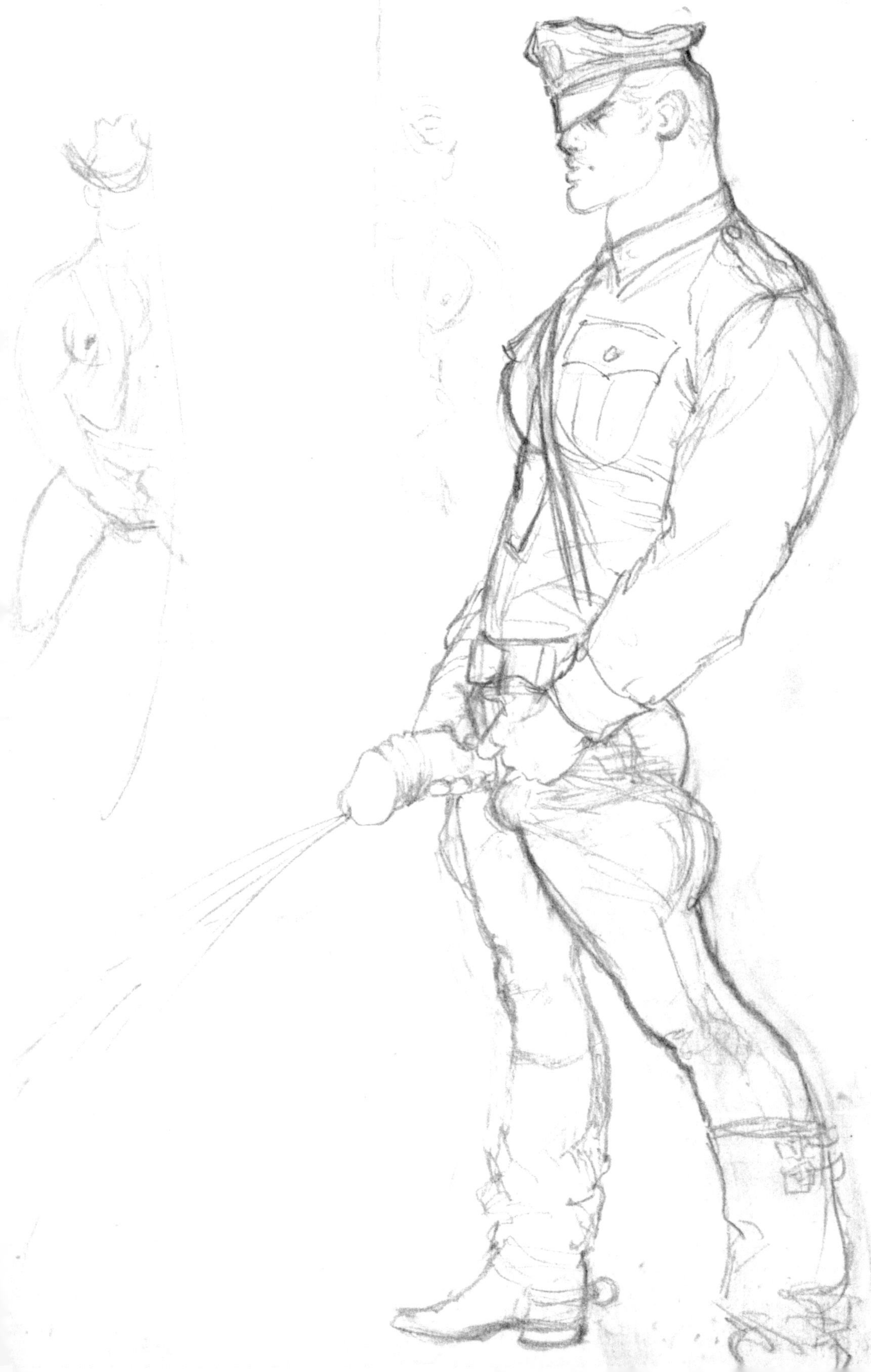

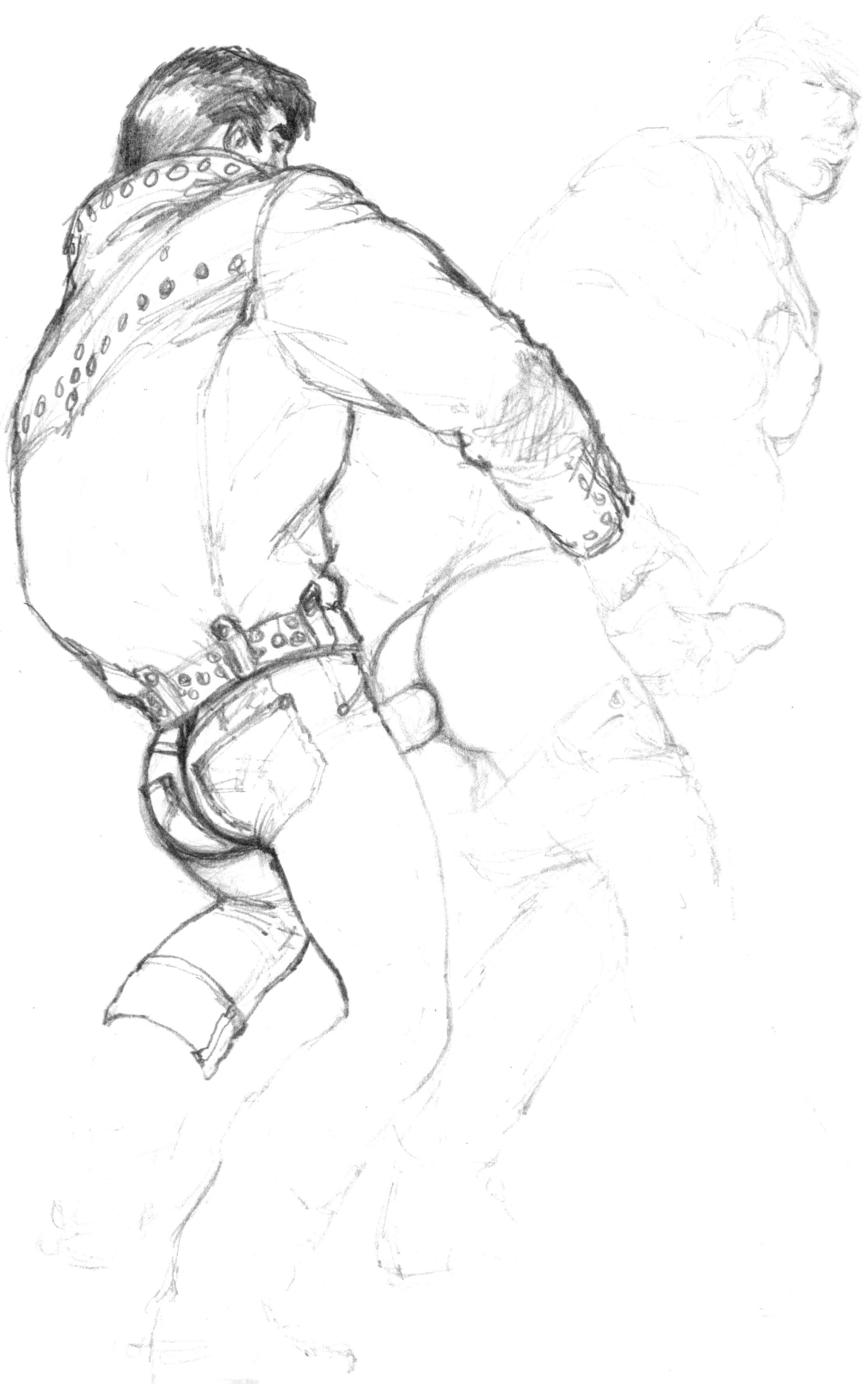

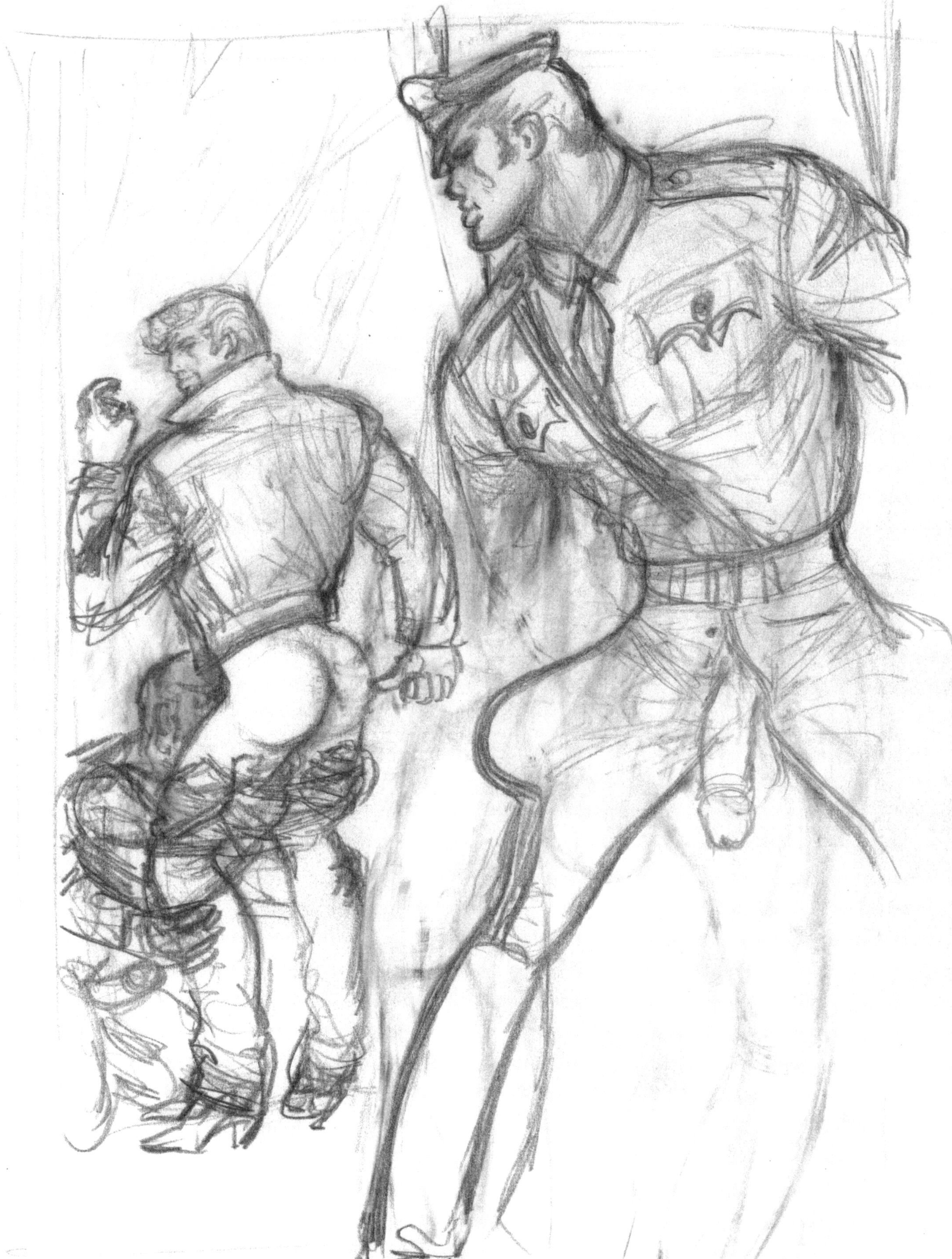

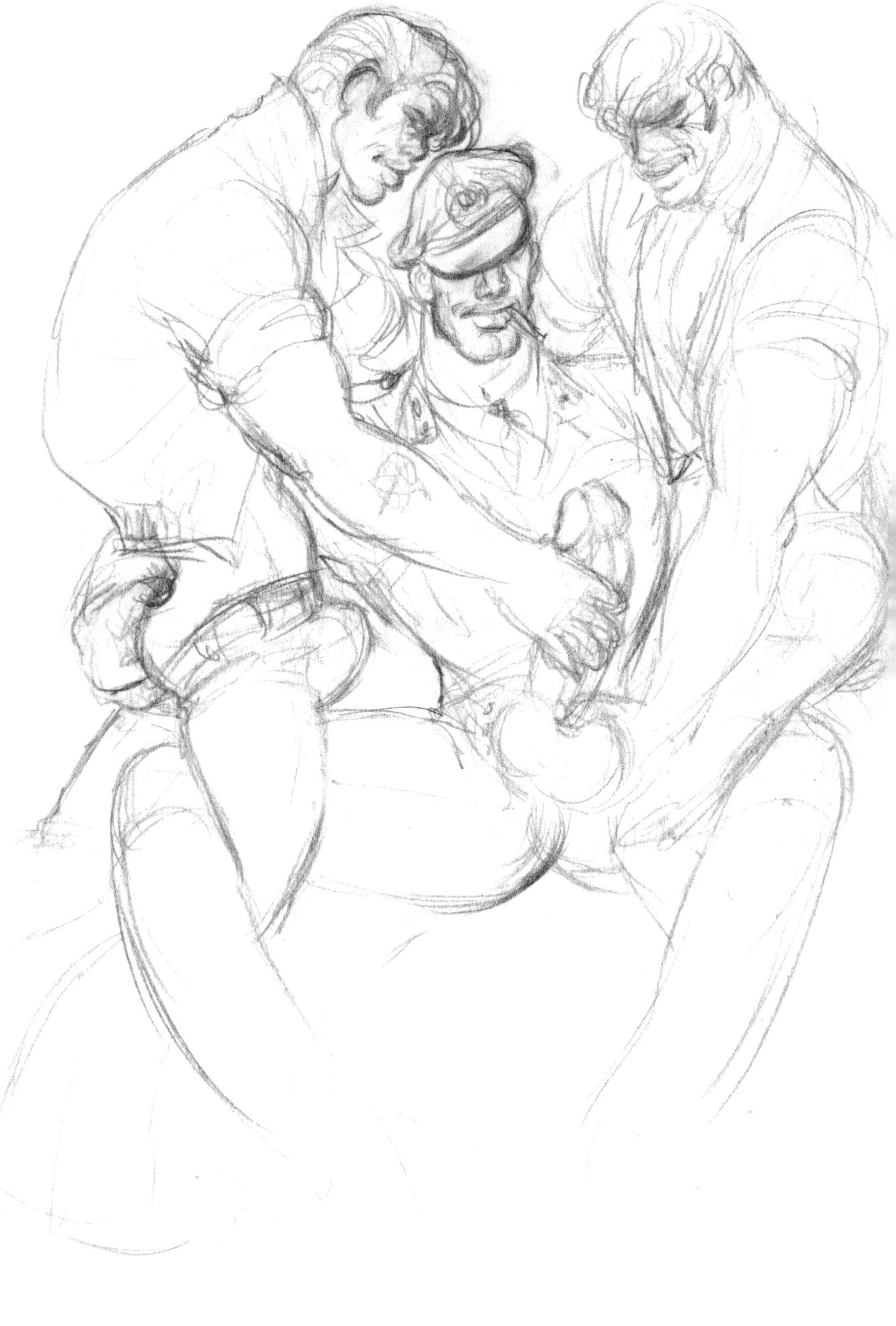

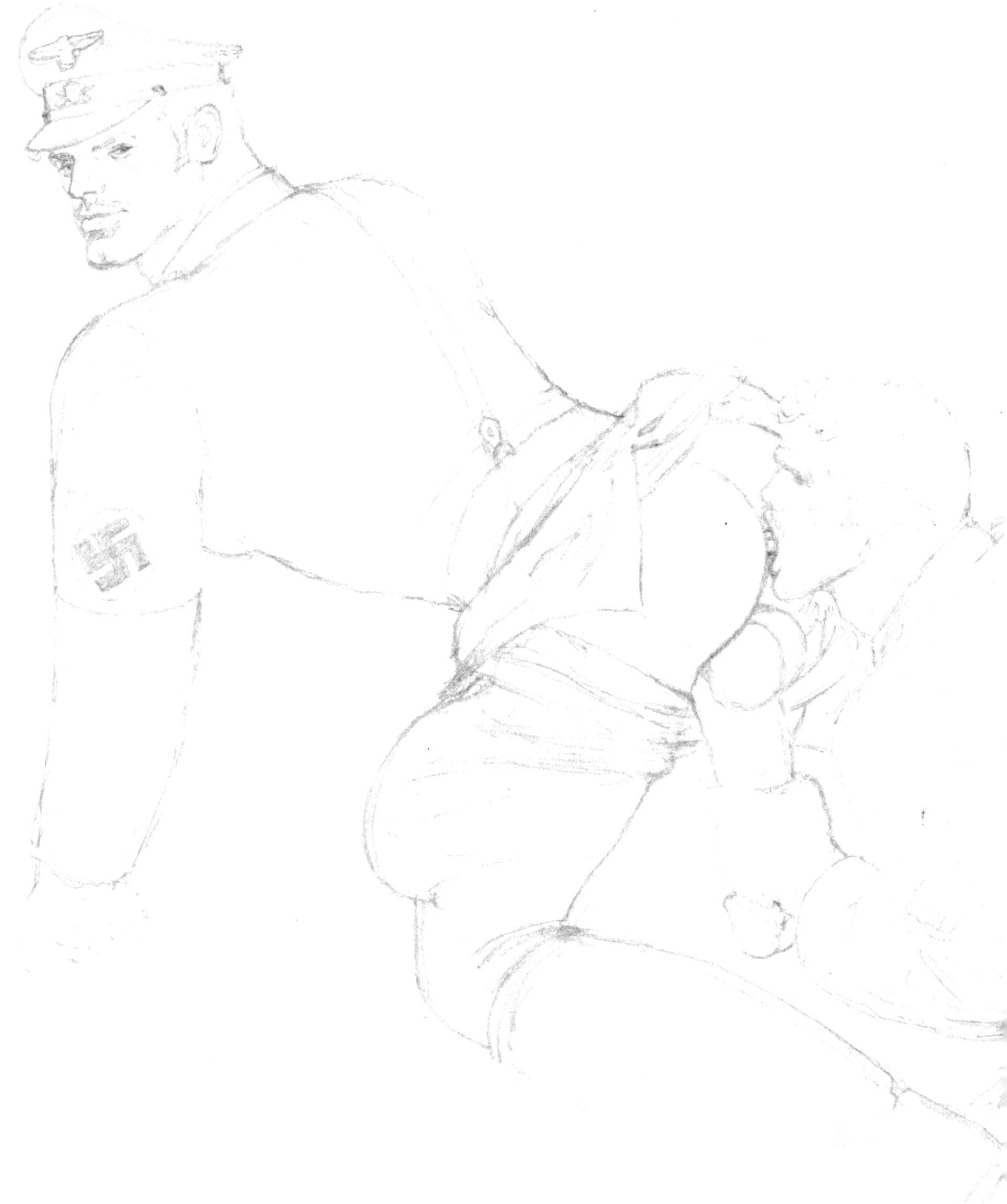

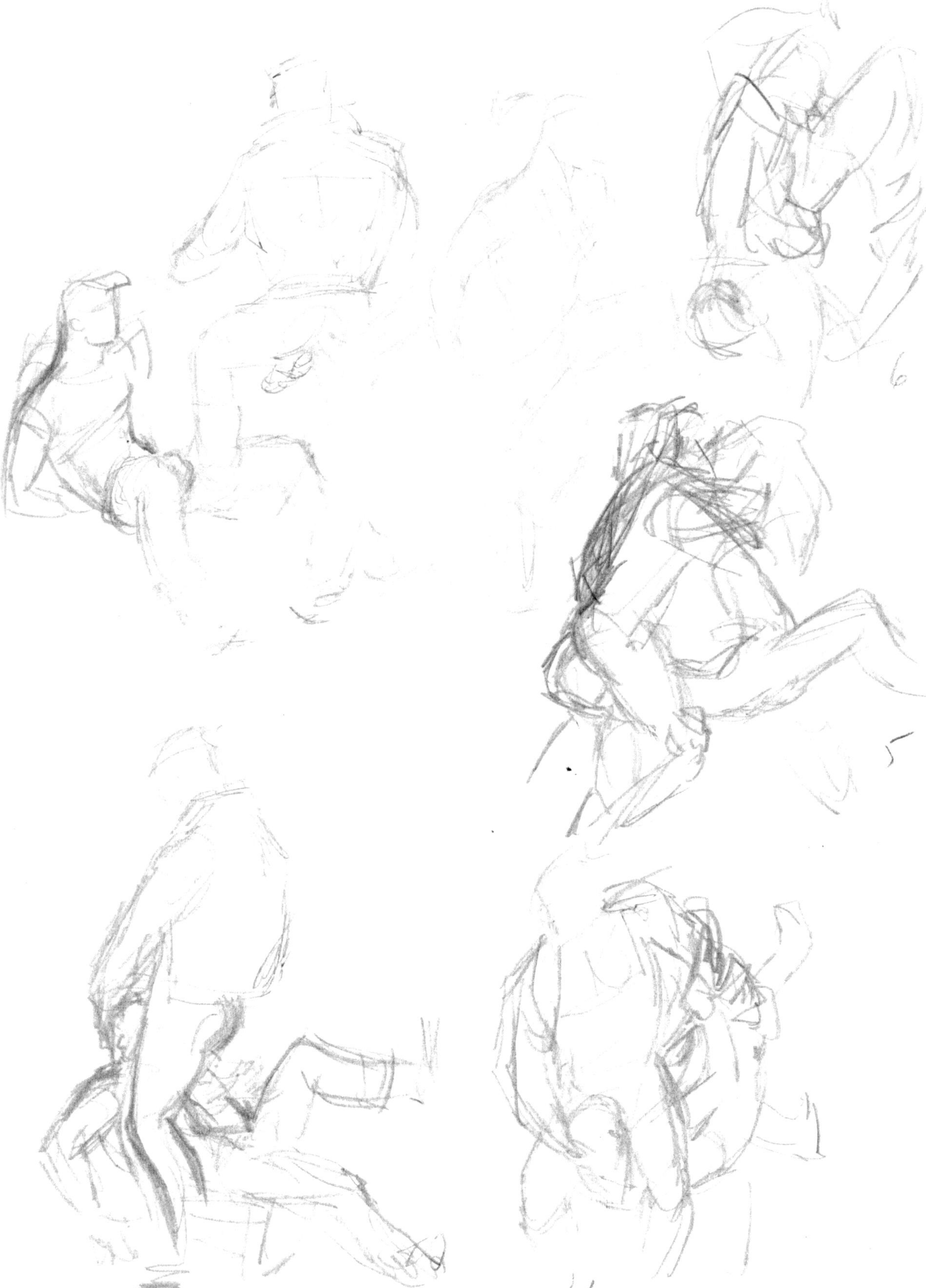

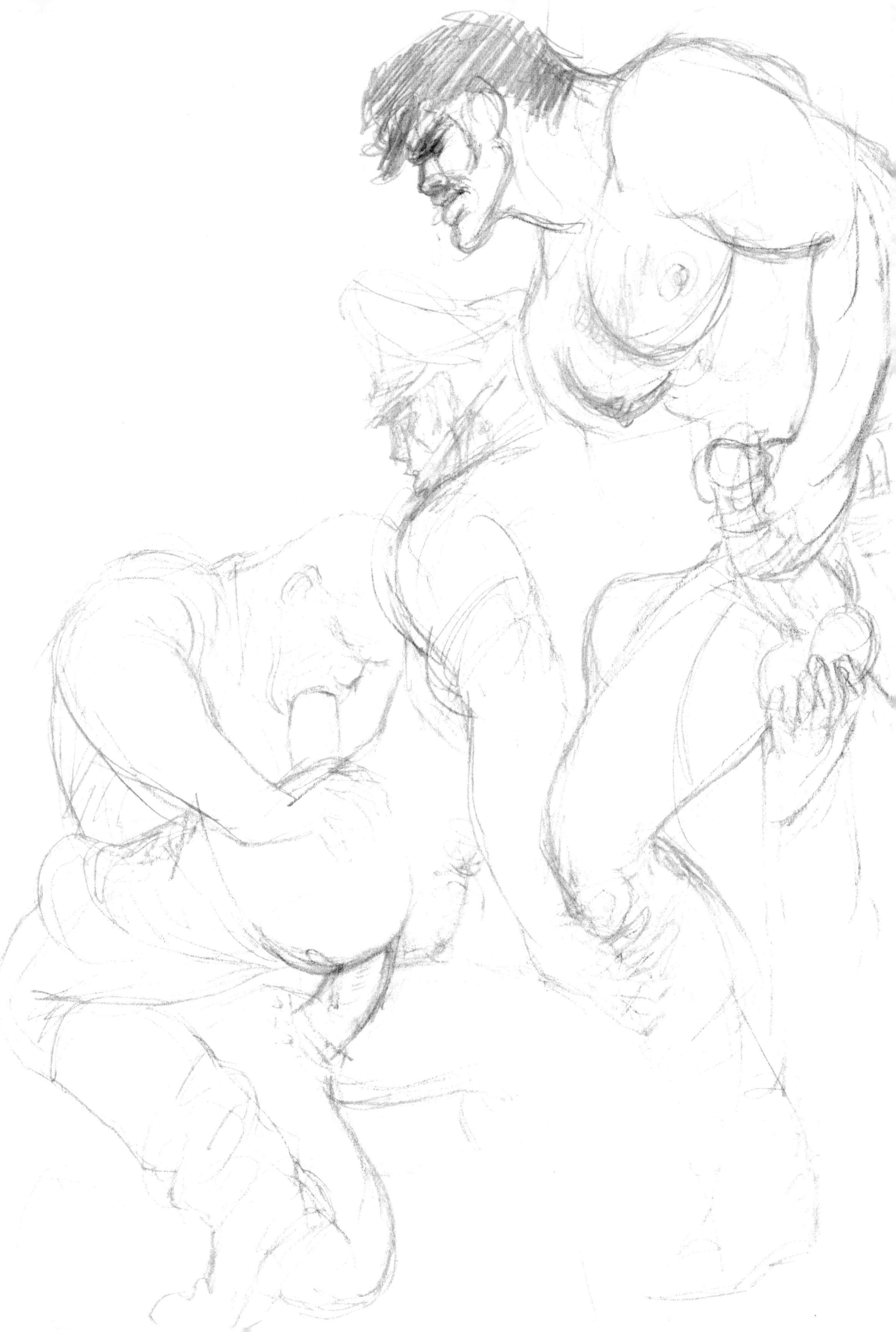

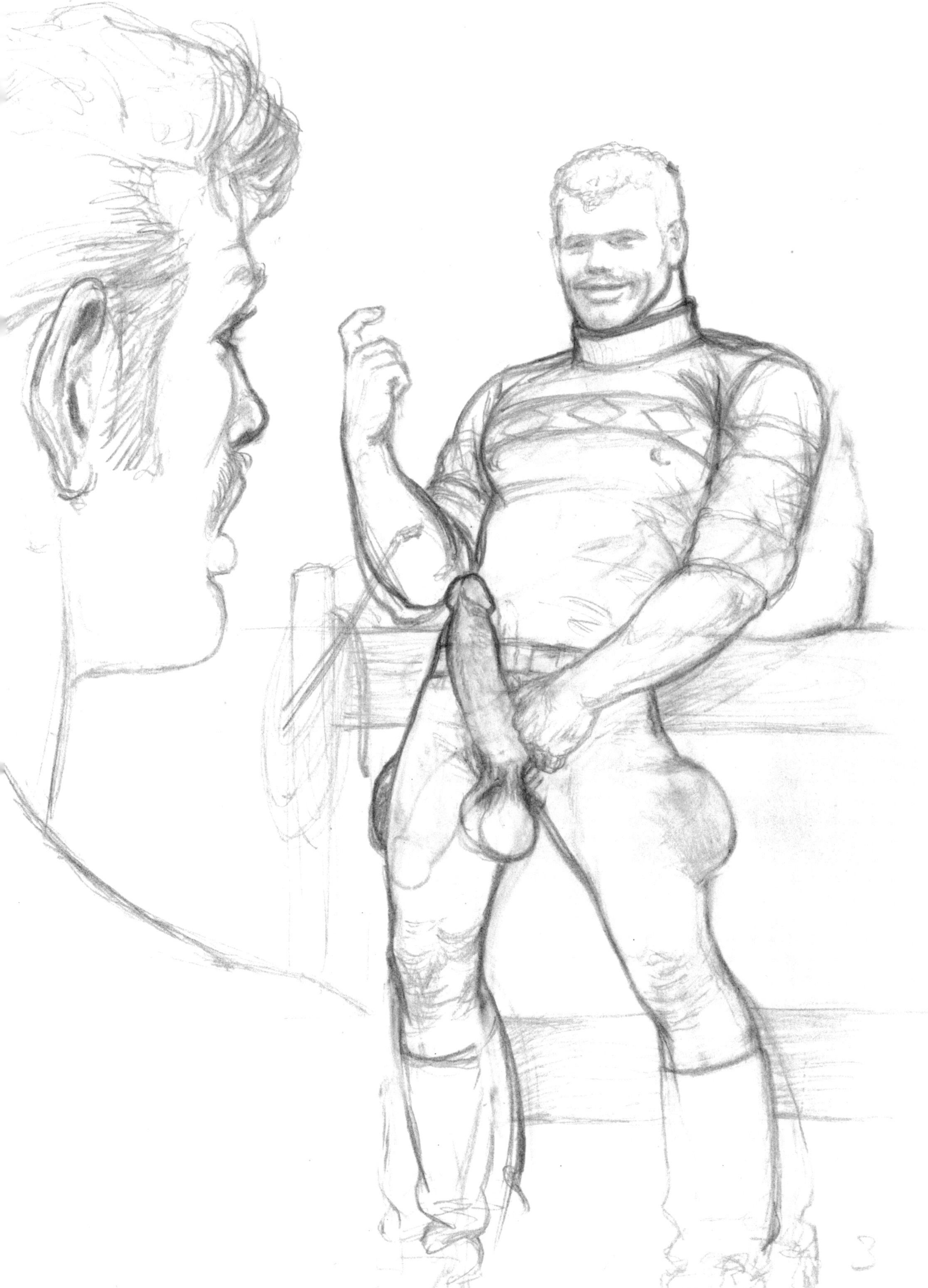

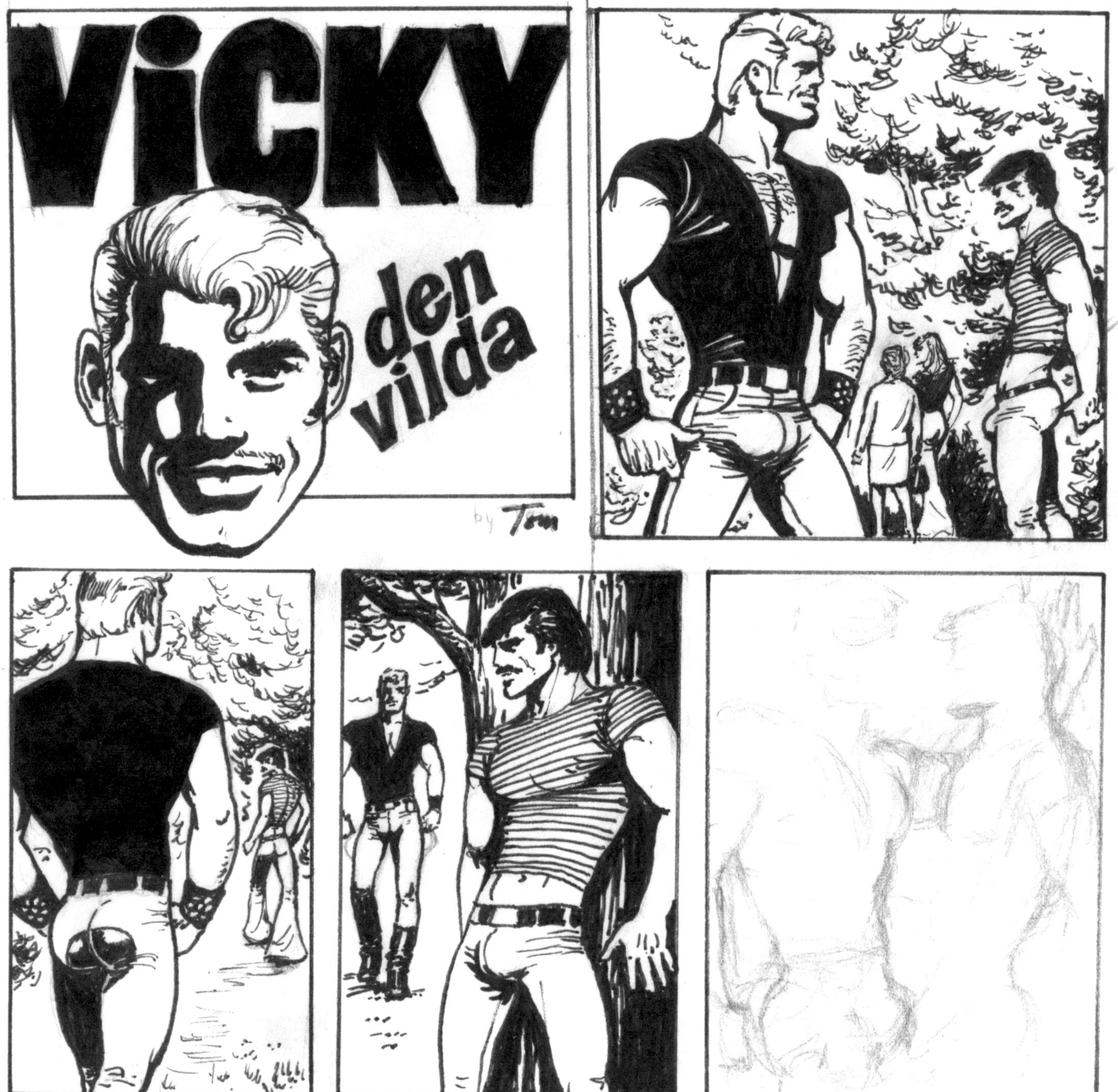
ViCKY
den vilda
by Tom

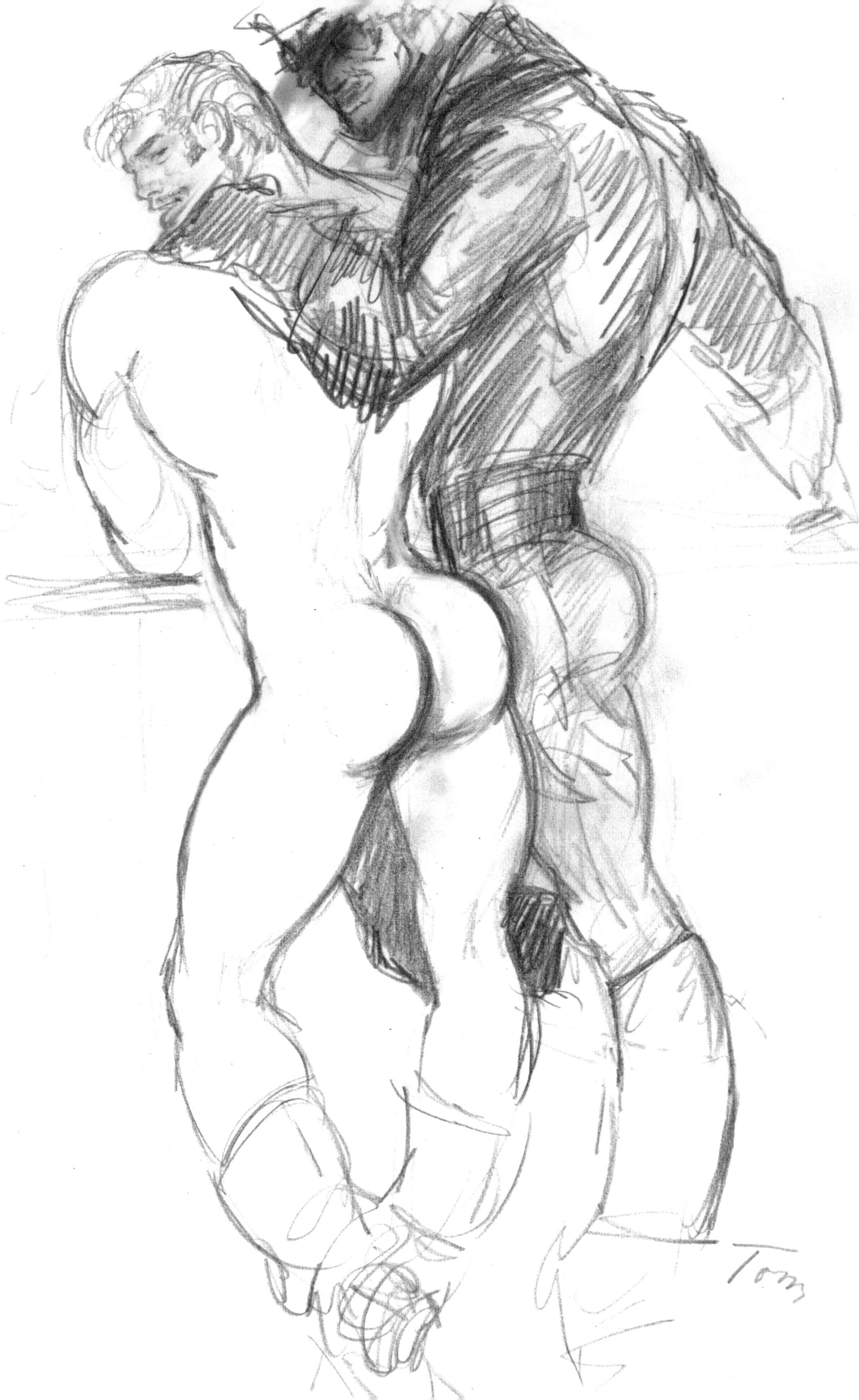
Tom

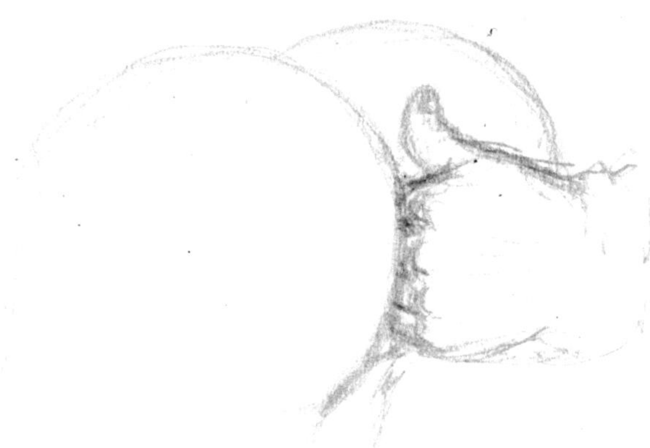

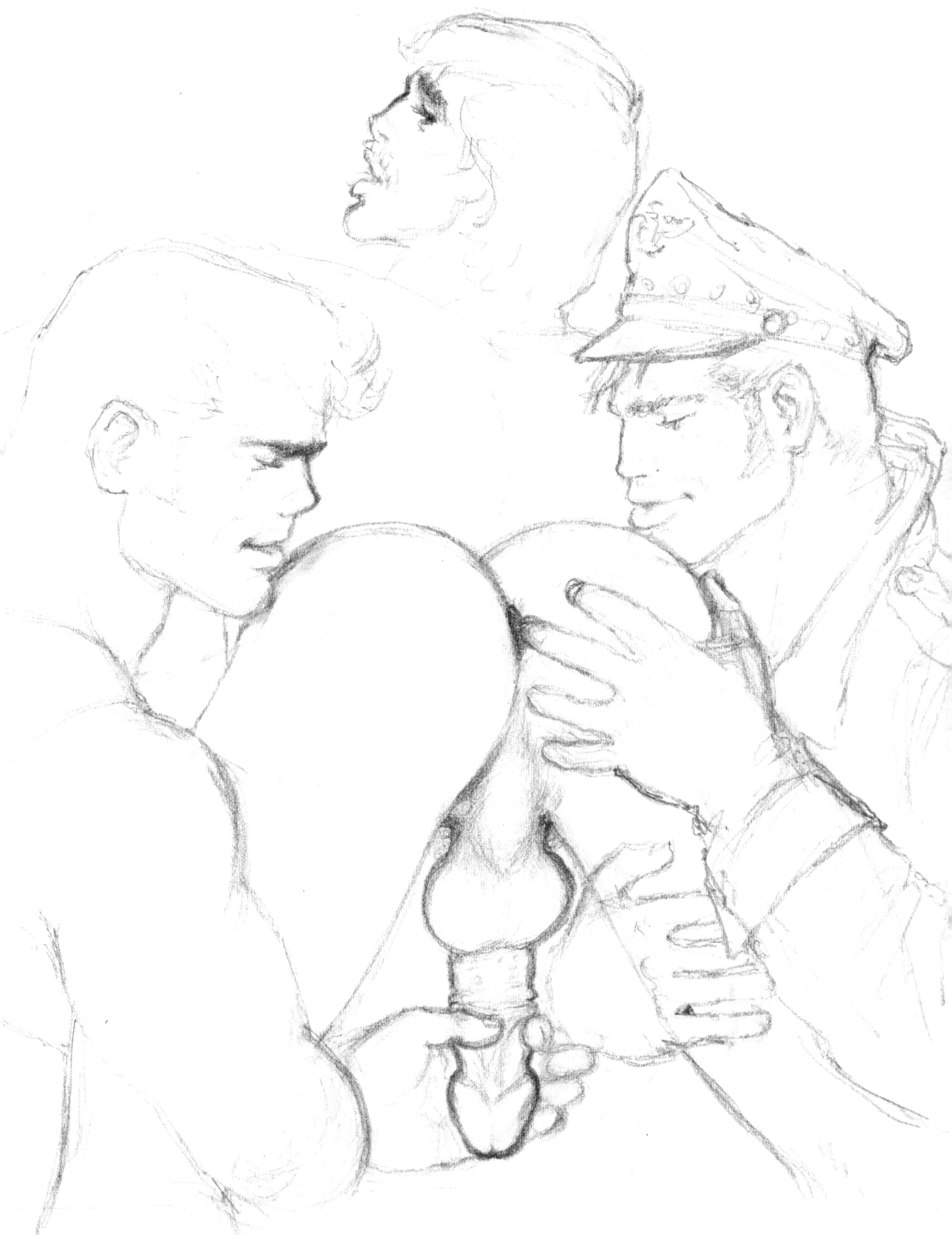

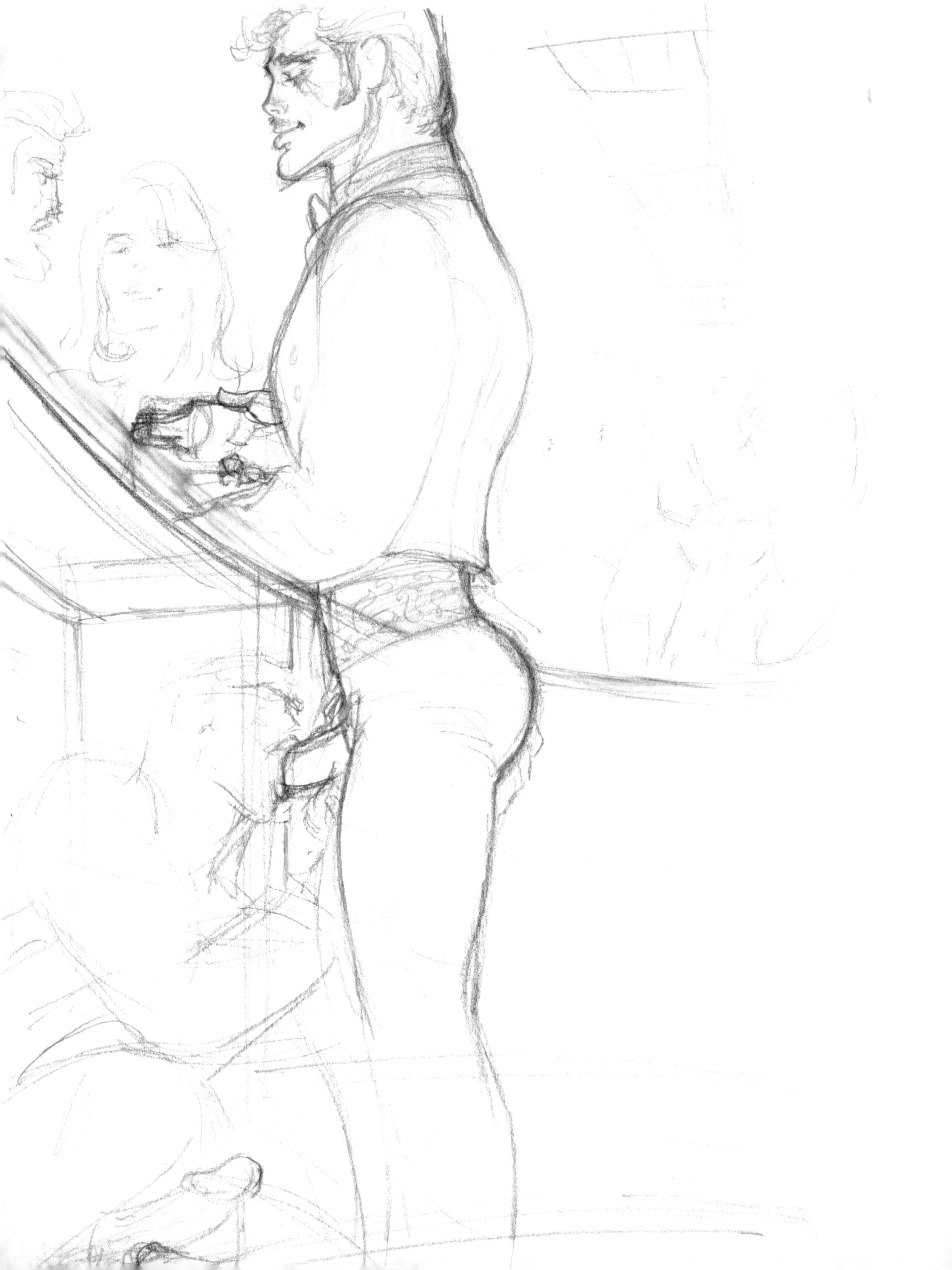

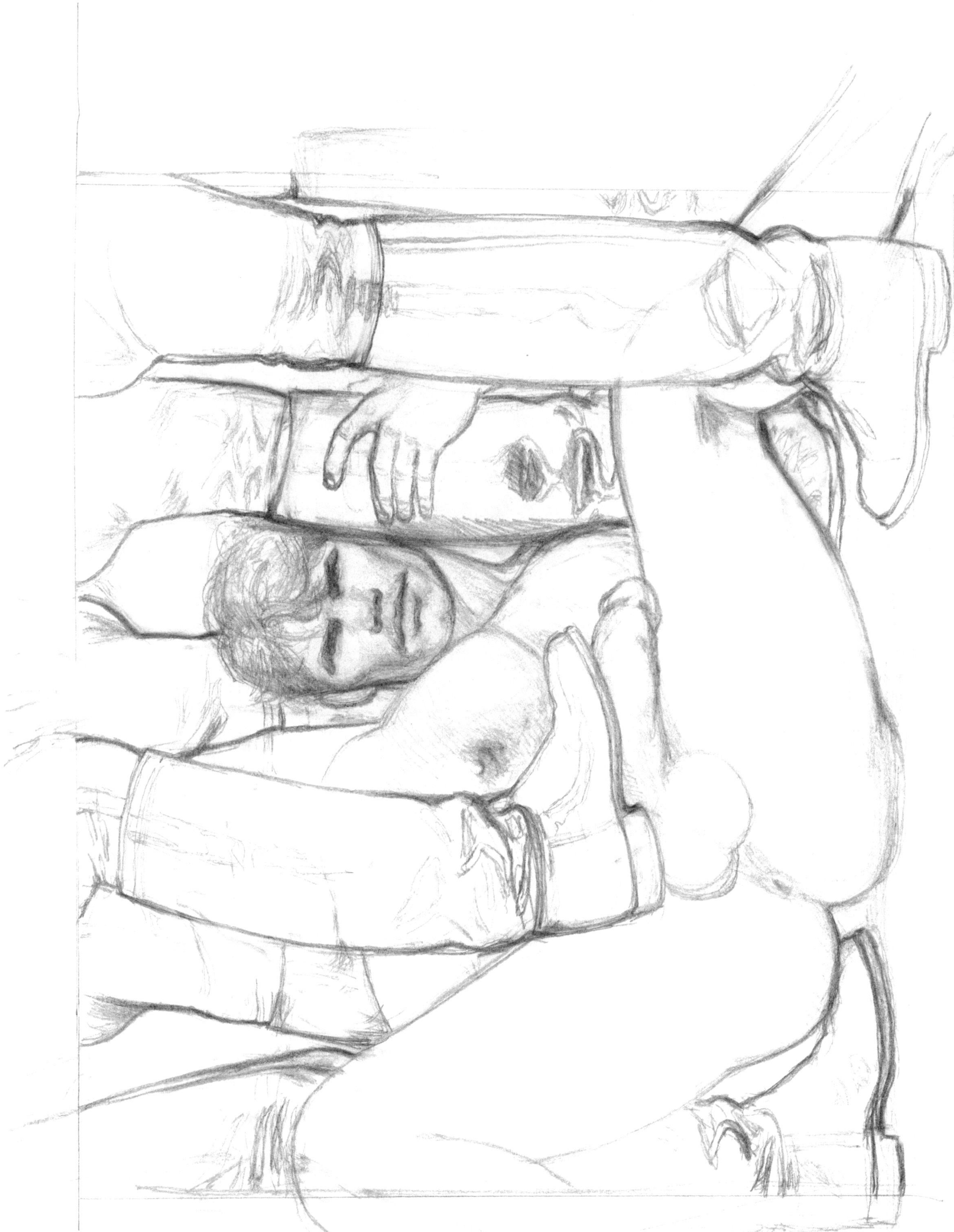

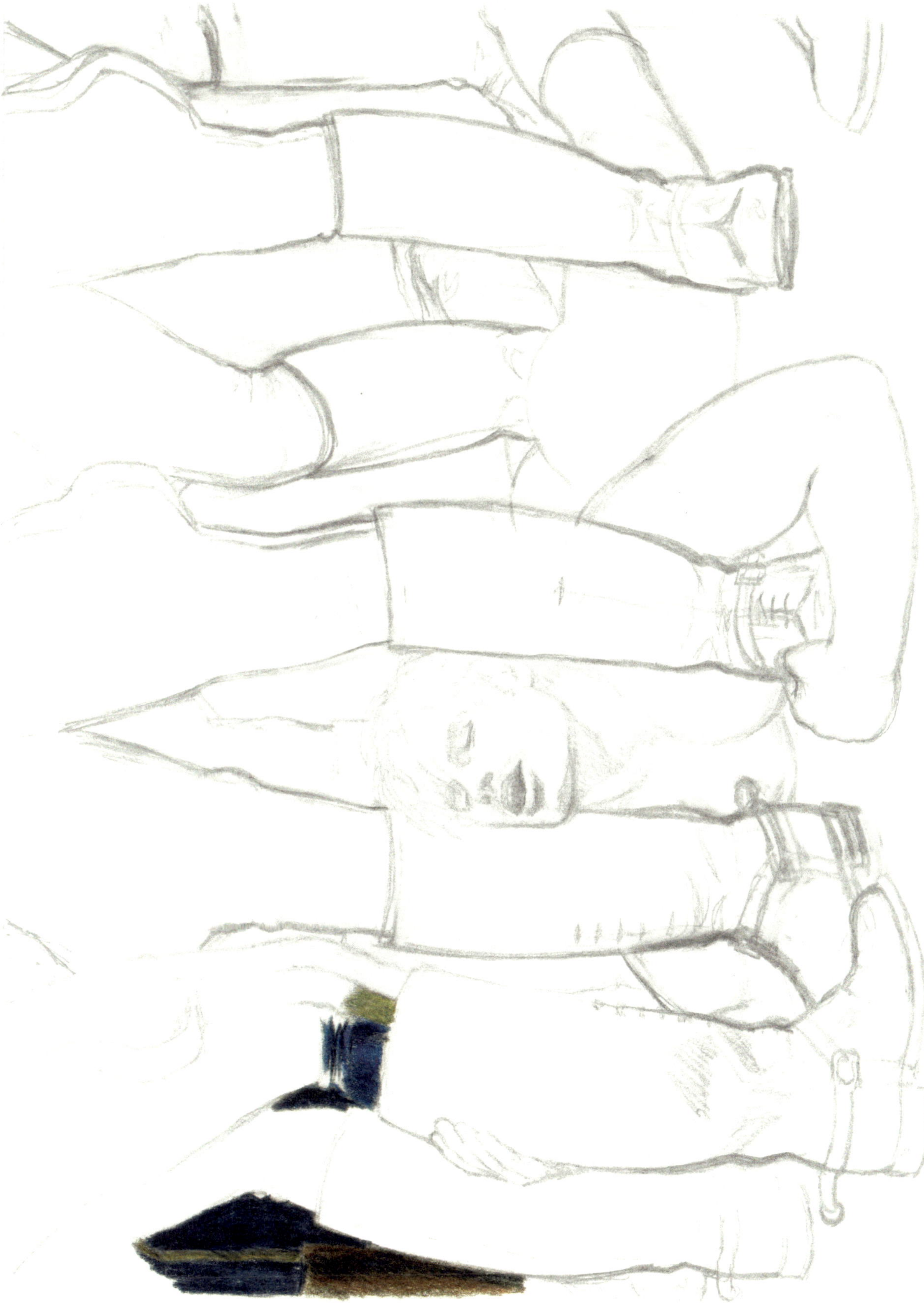

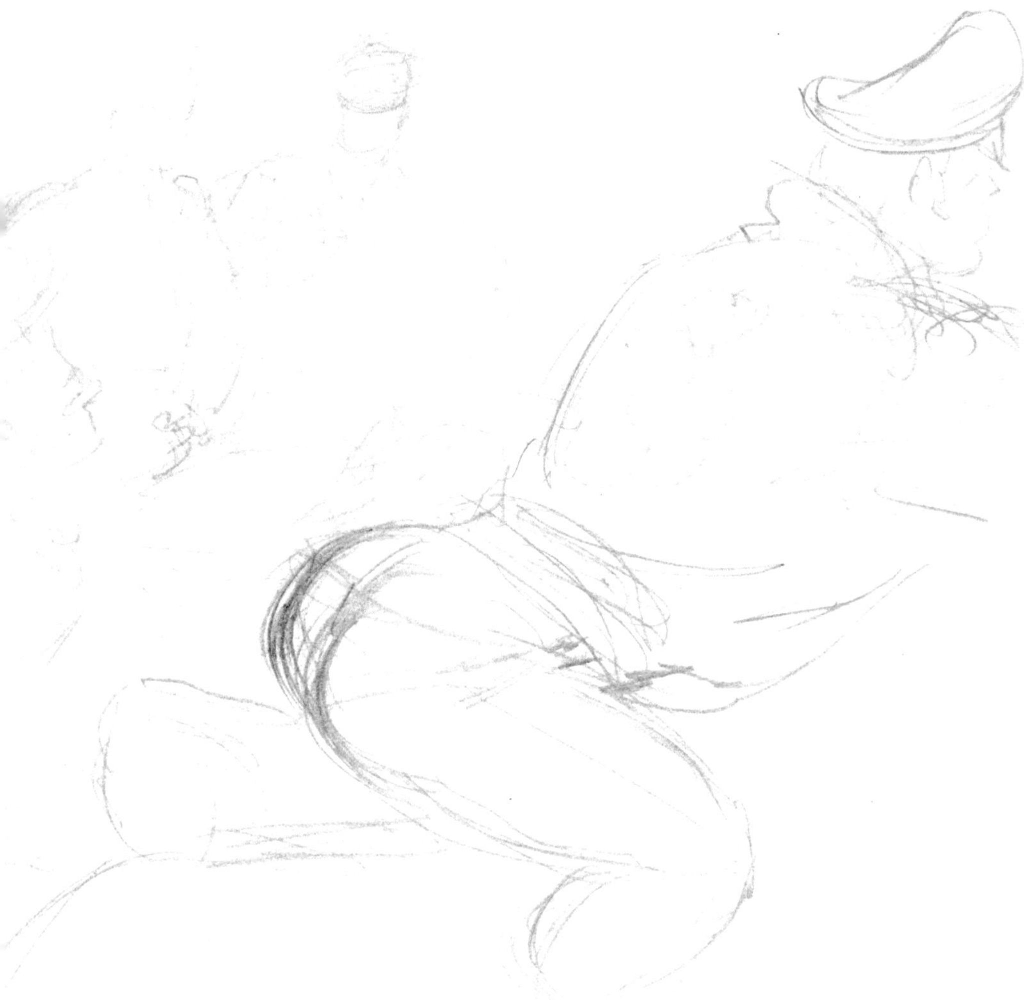

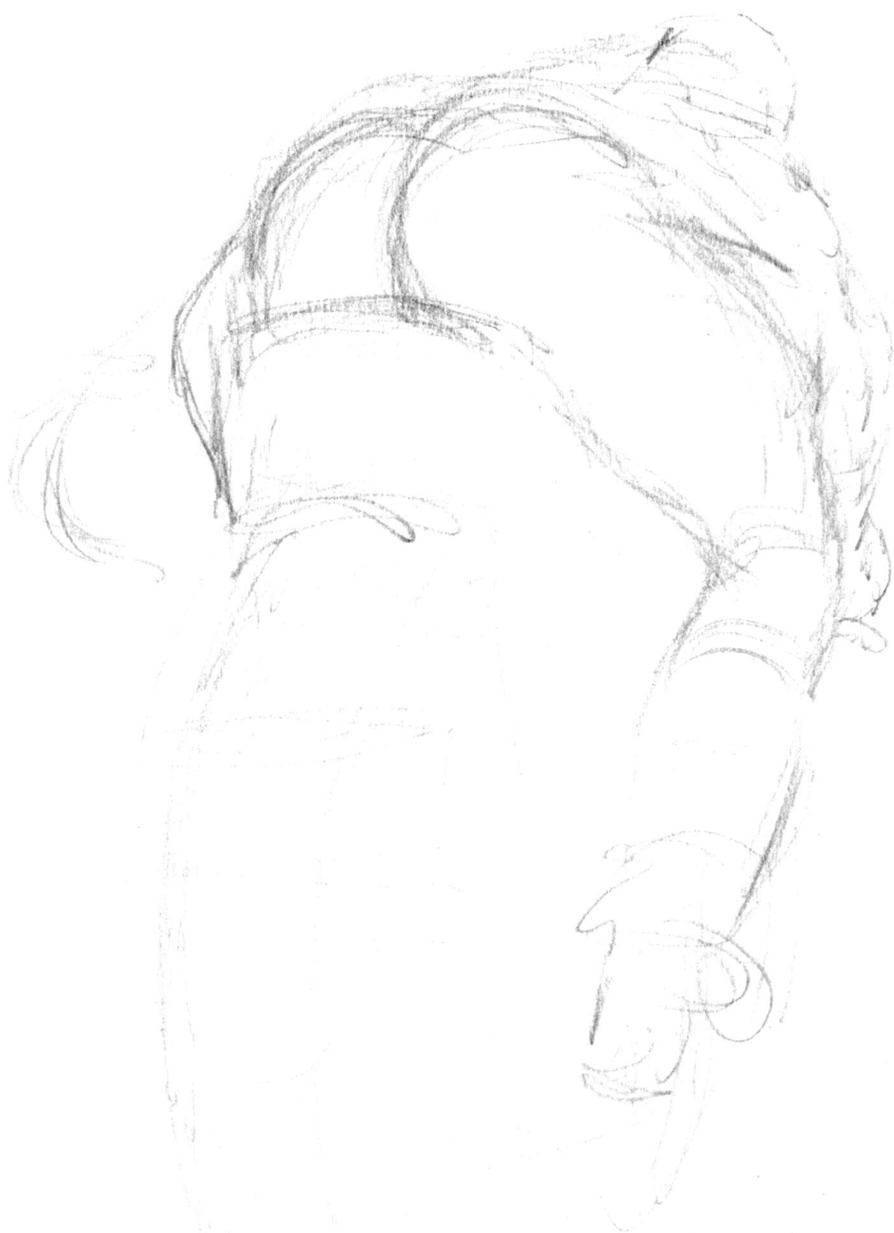

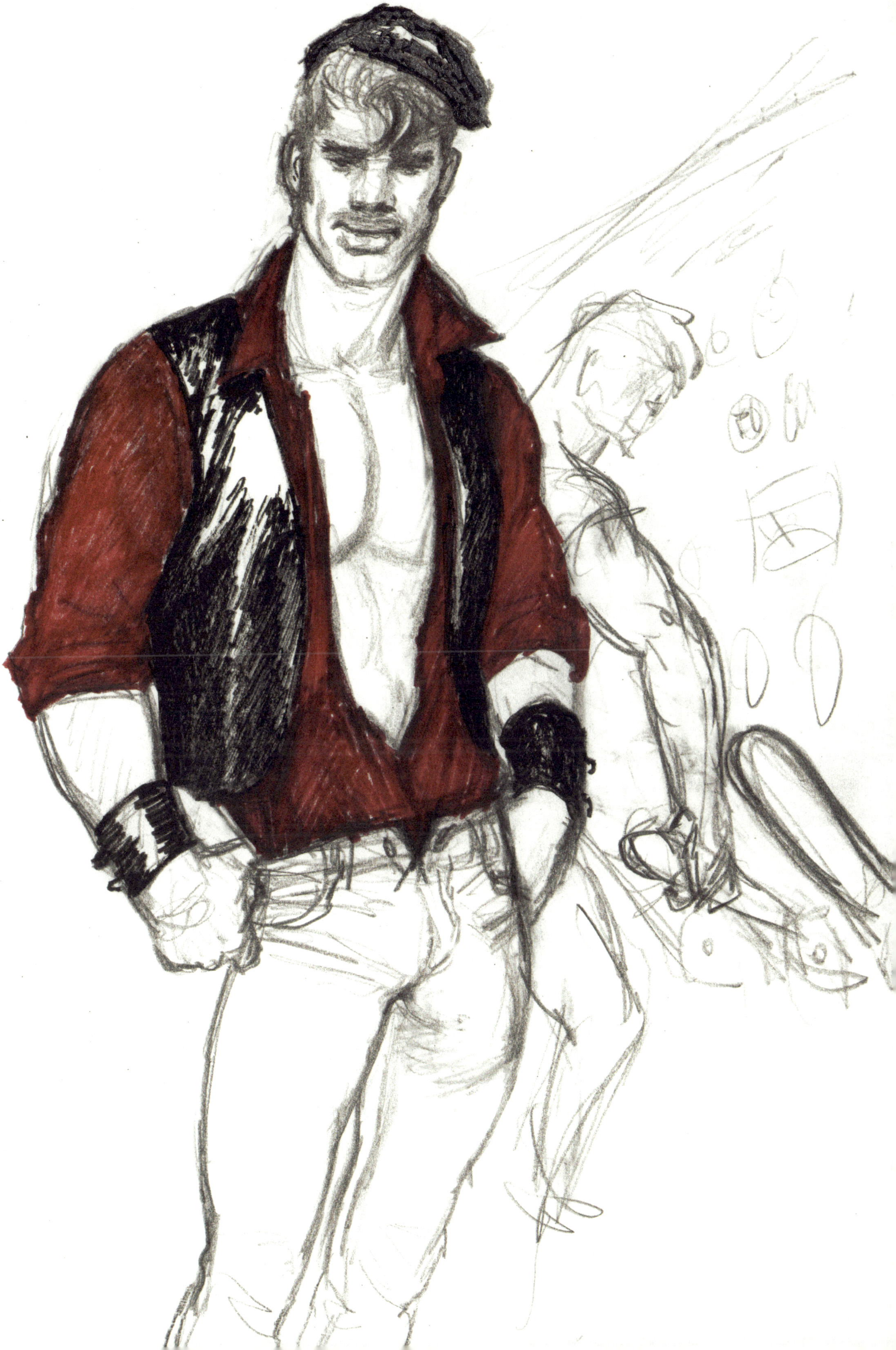

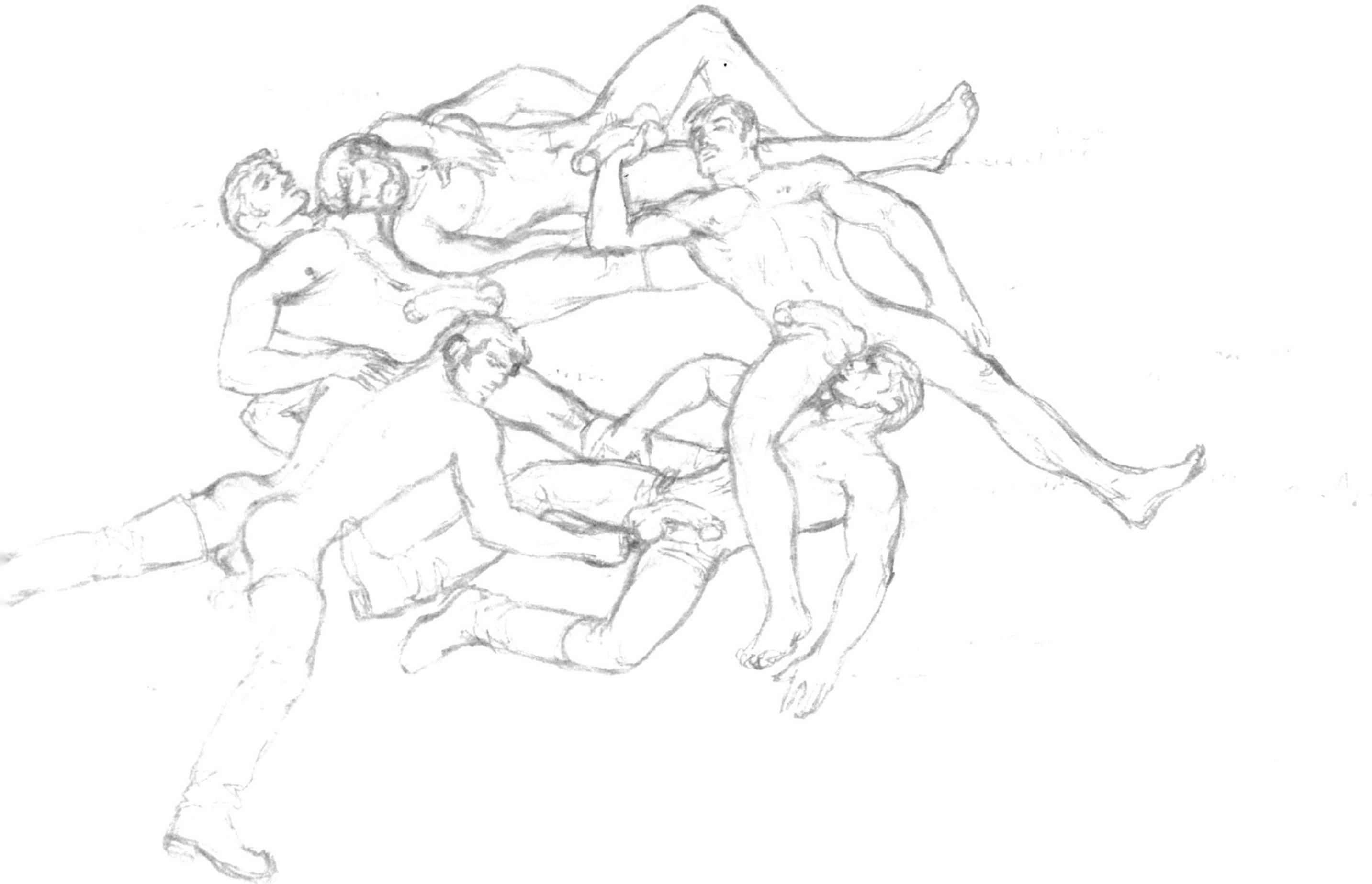

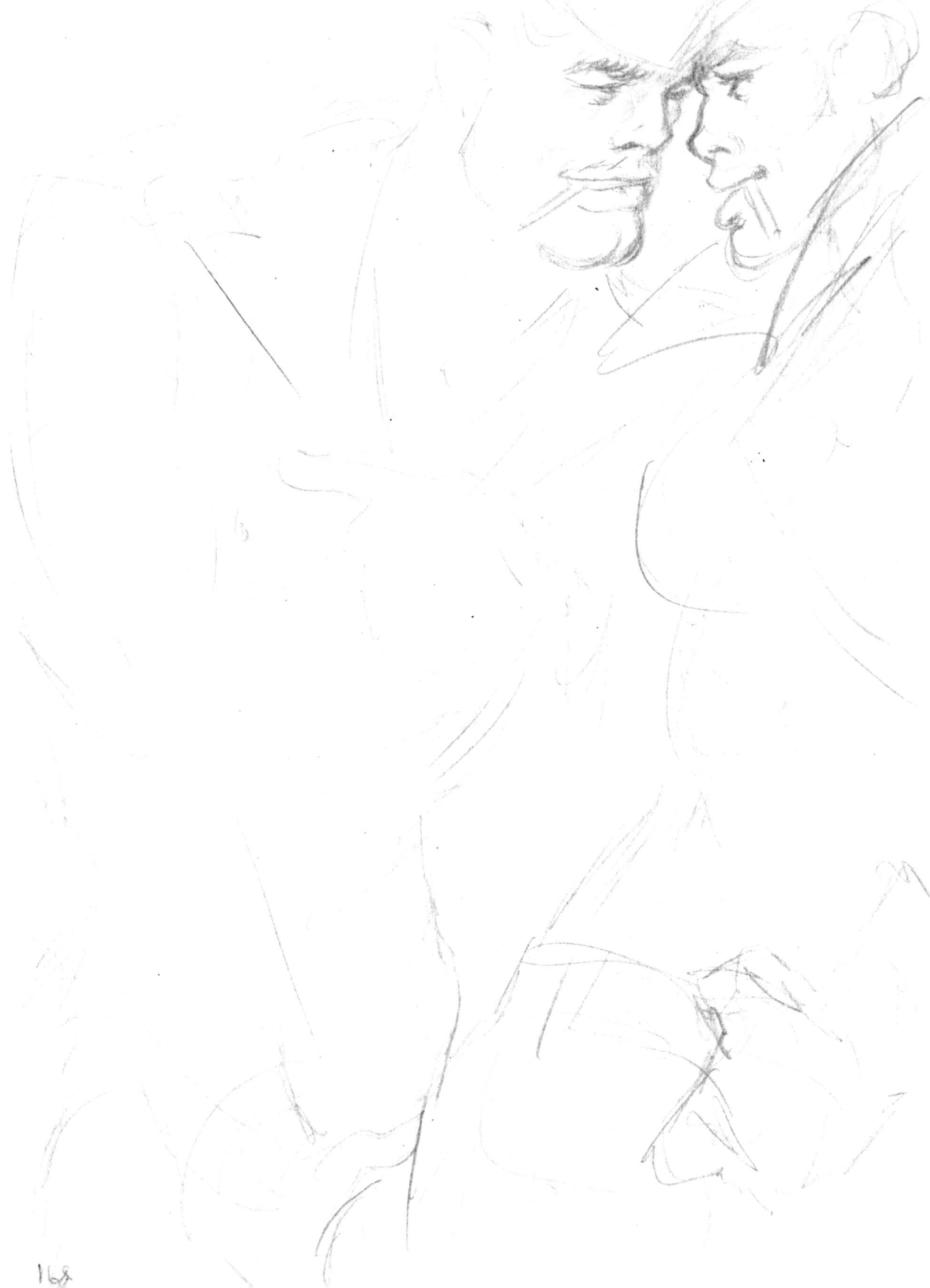

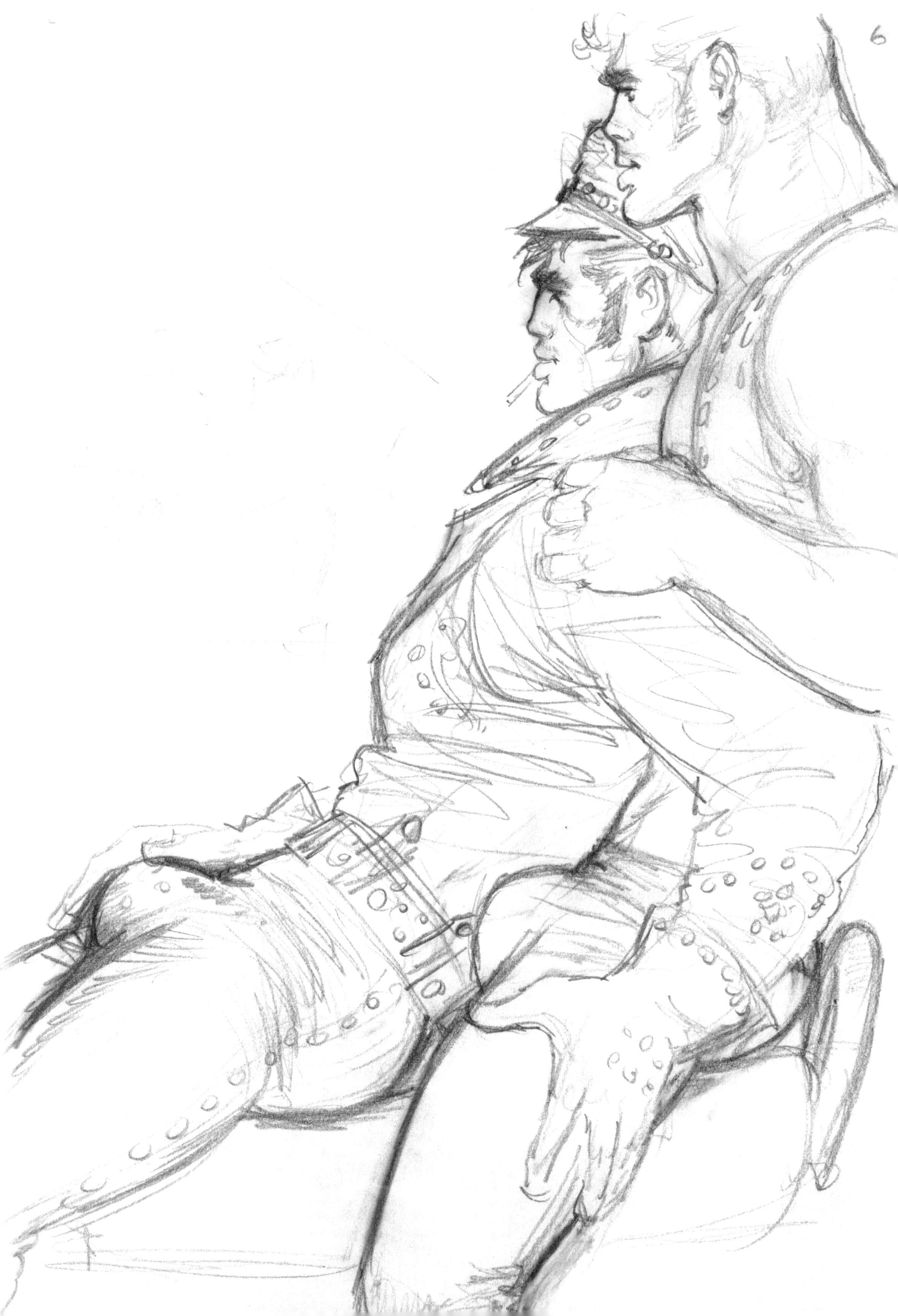

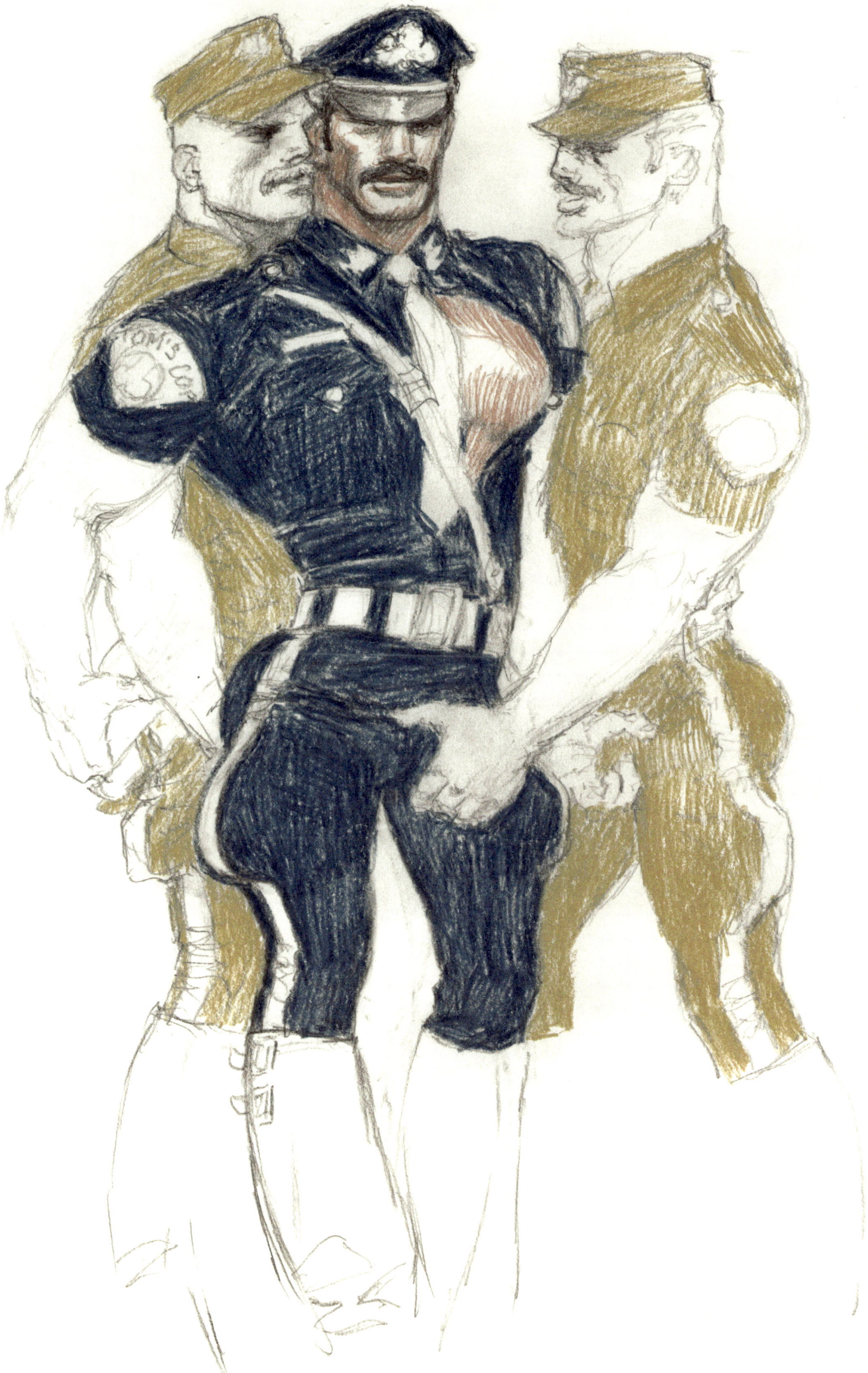

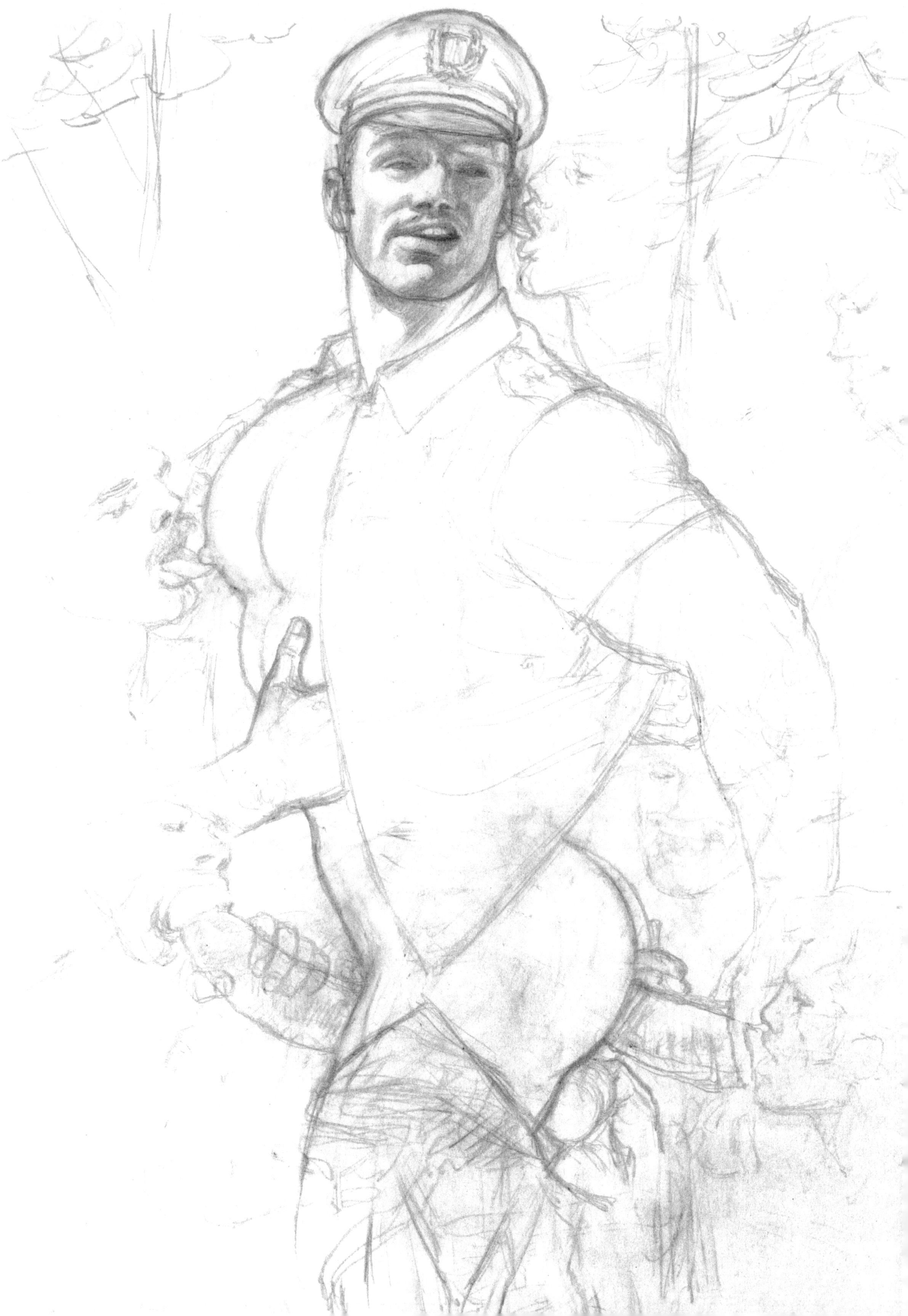

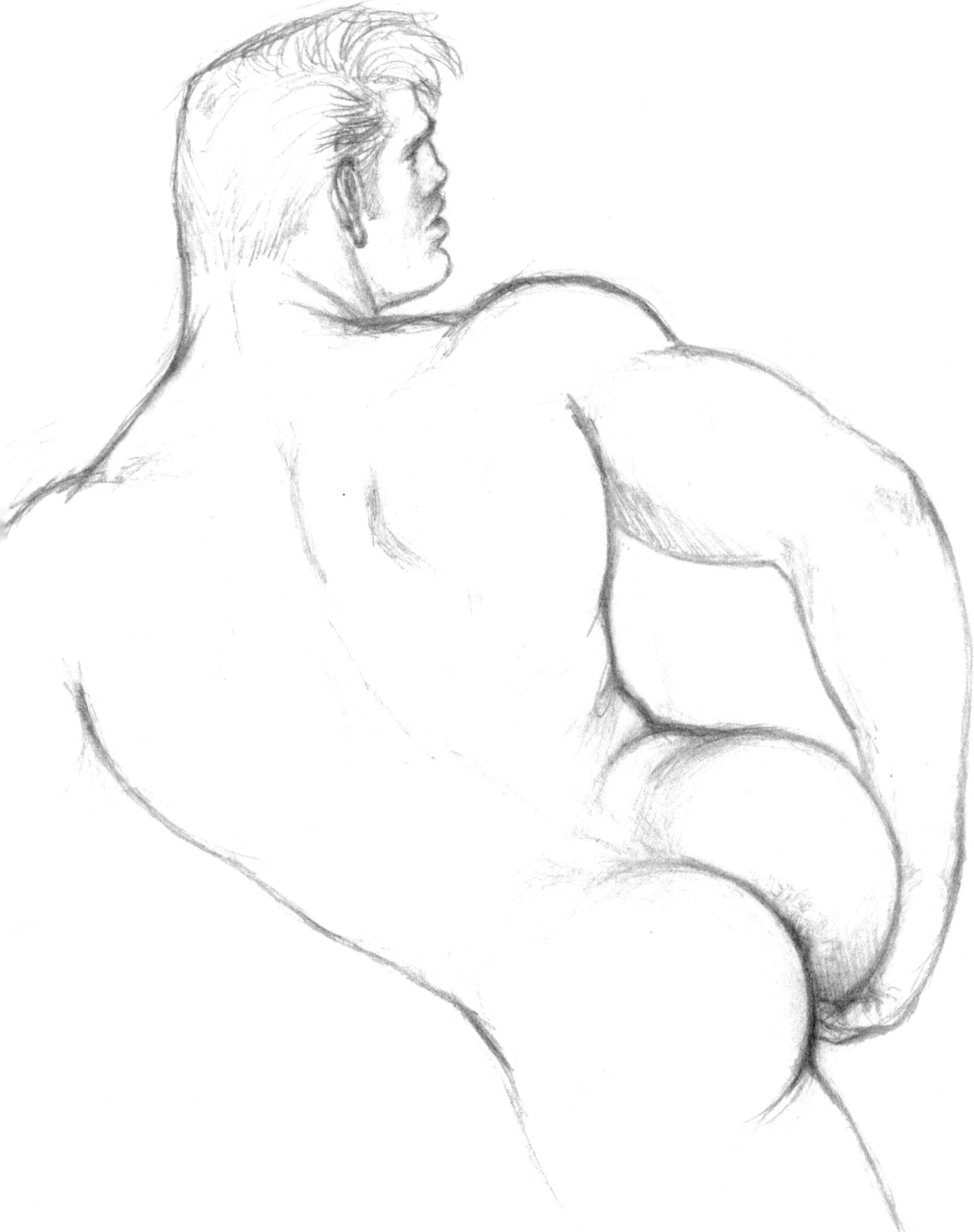

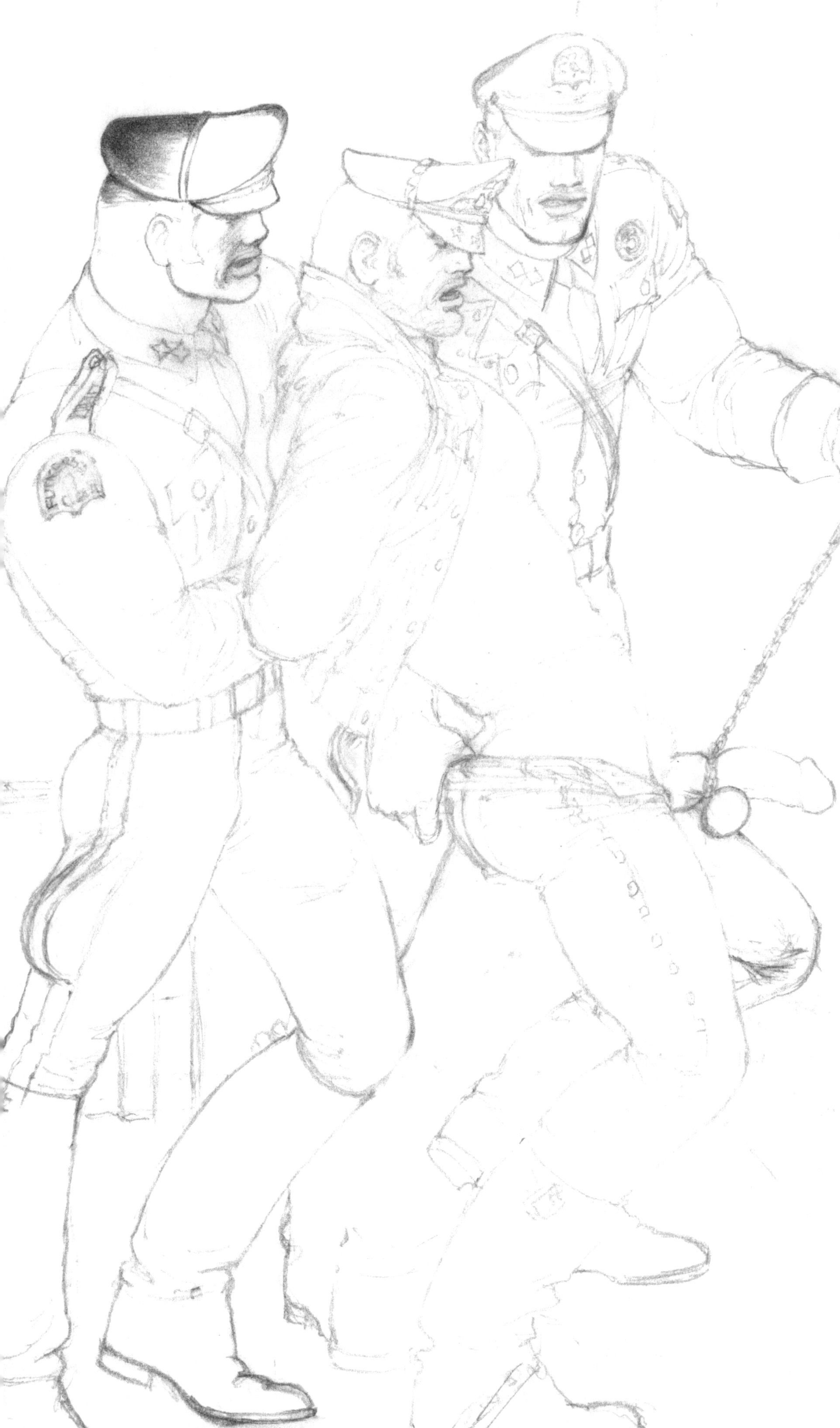

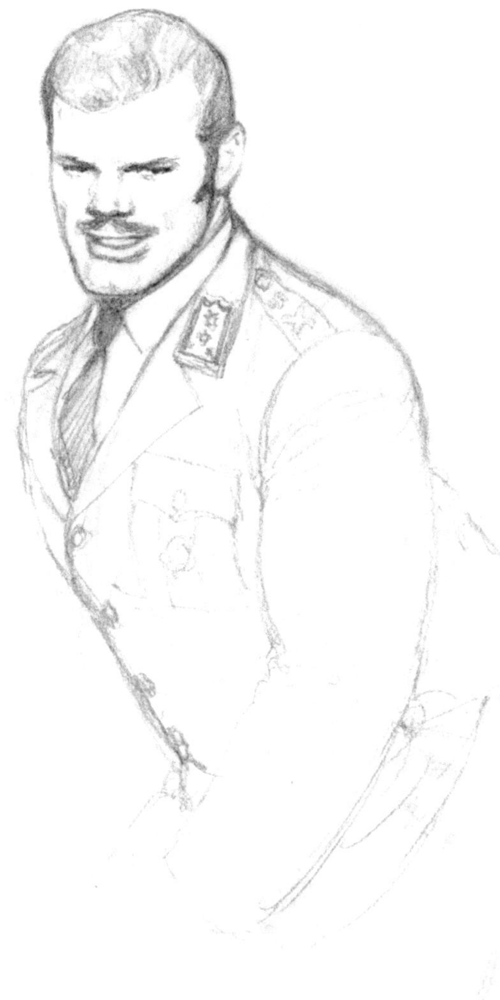

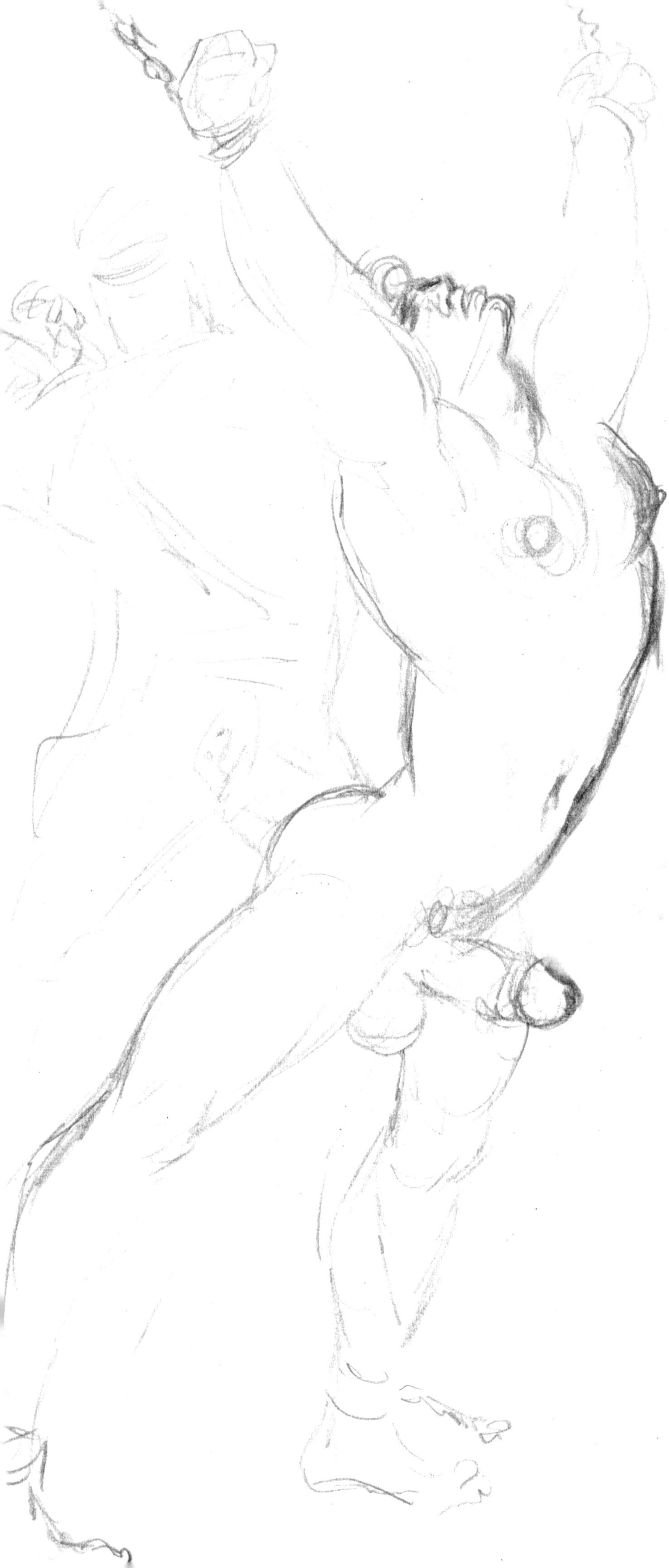

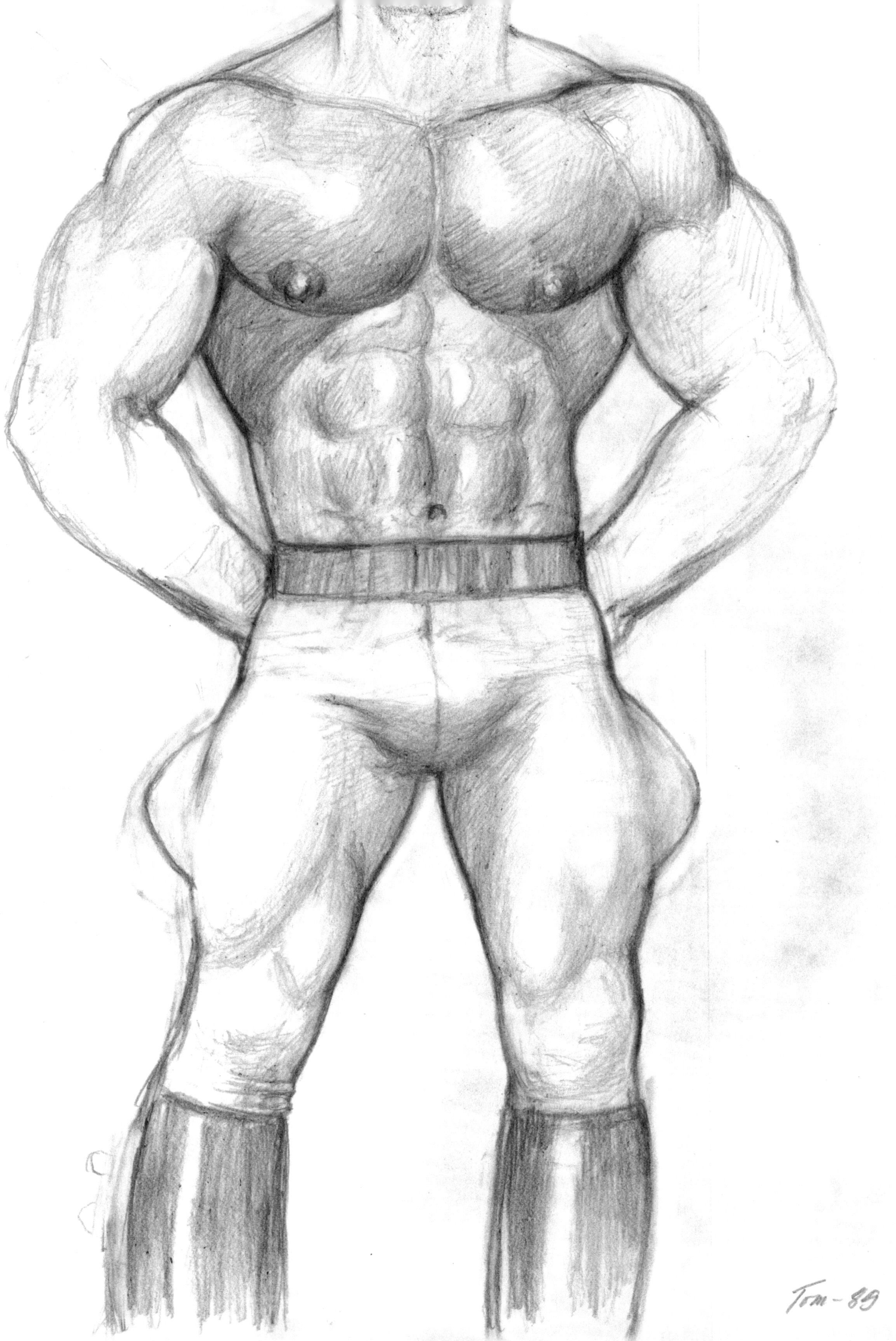
Tom-89

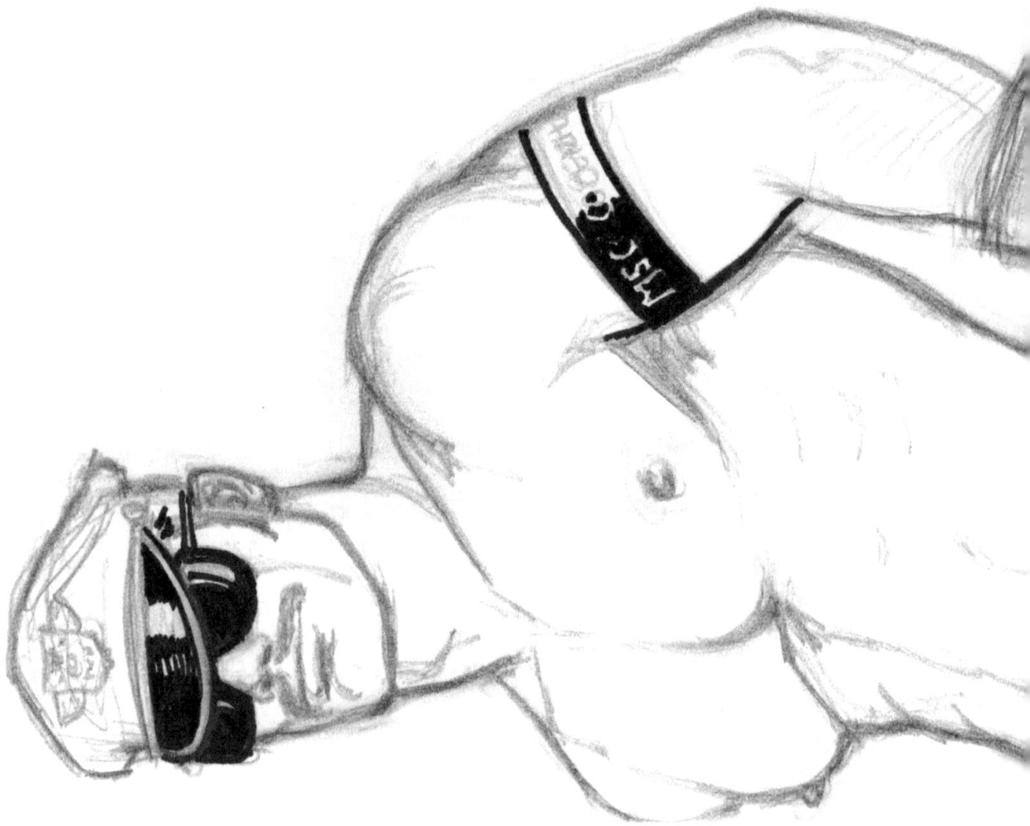

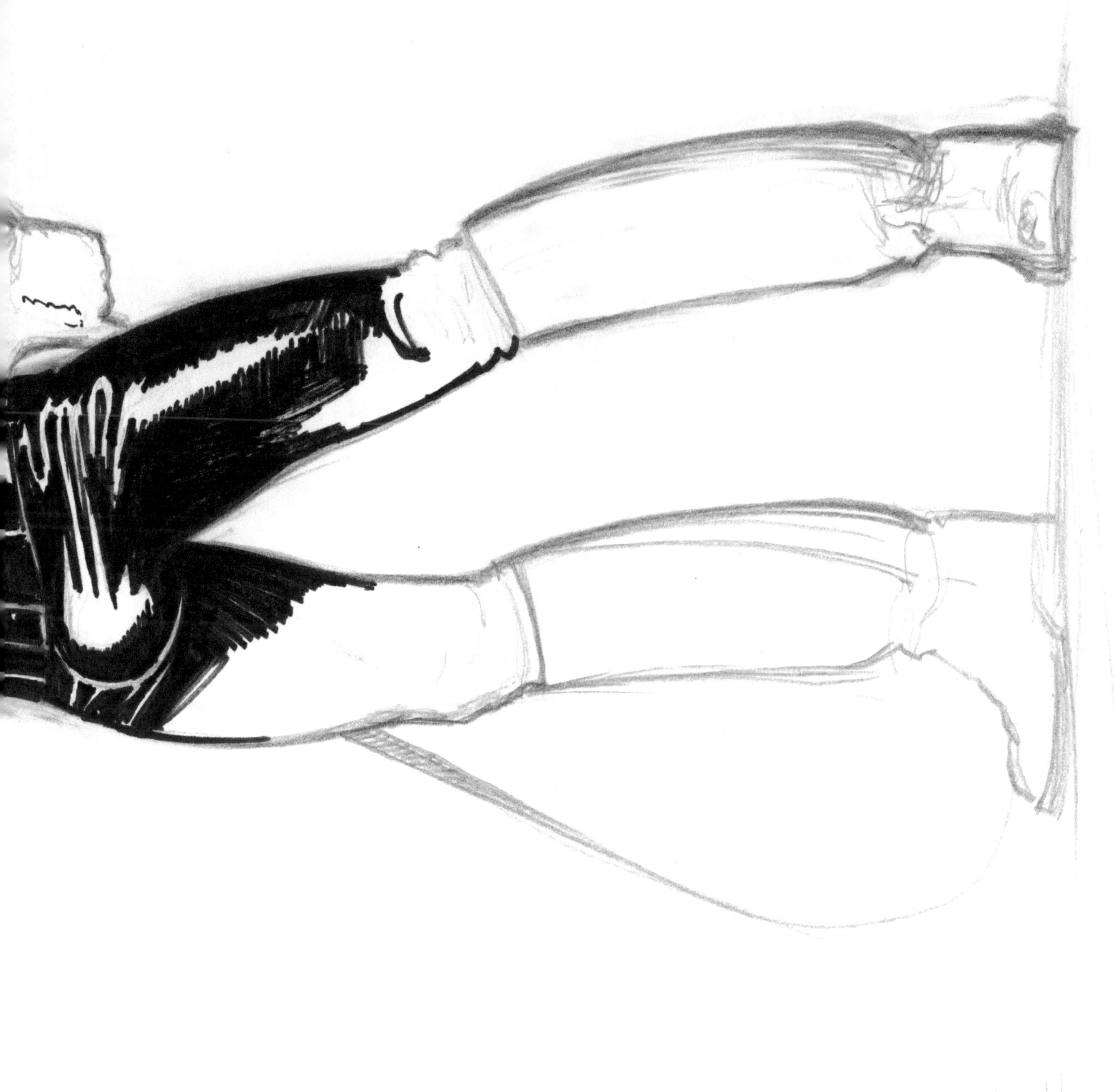

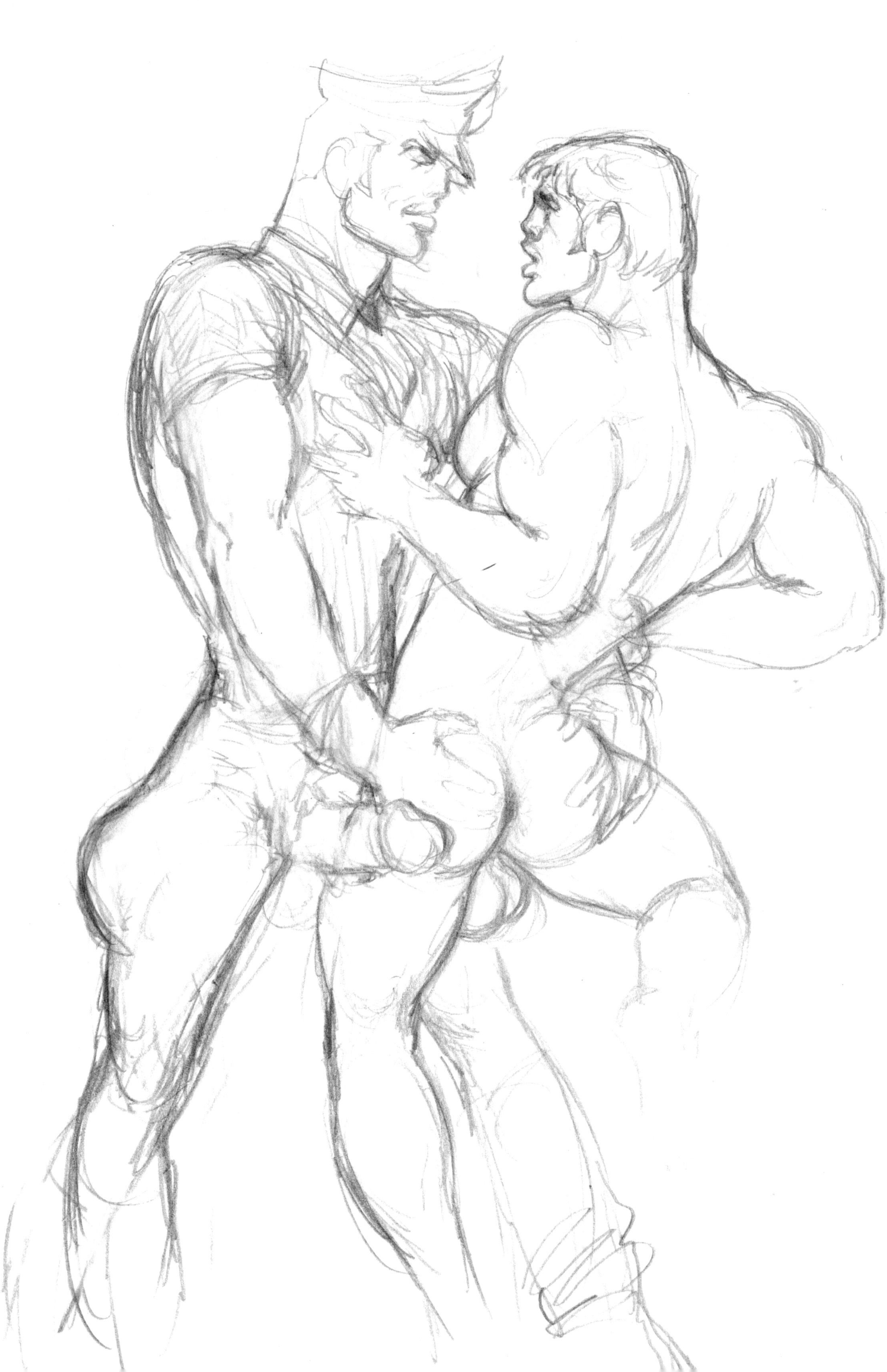

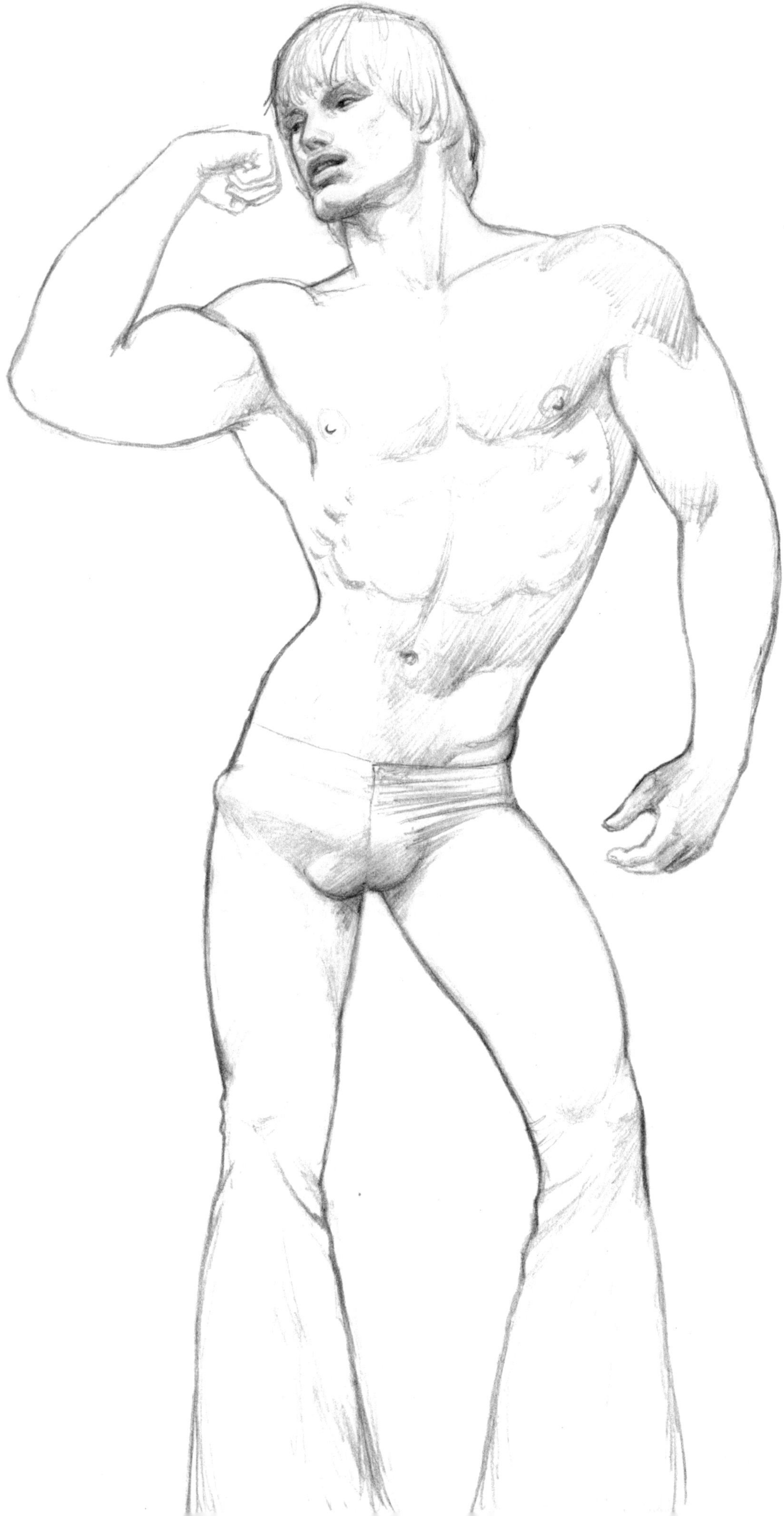

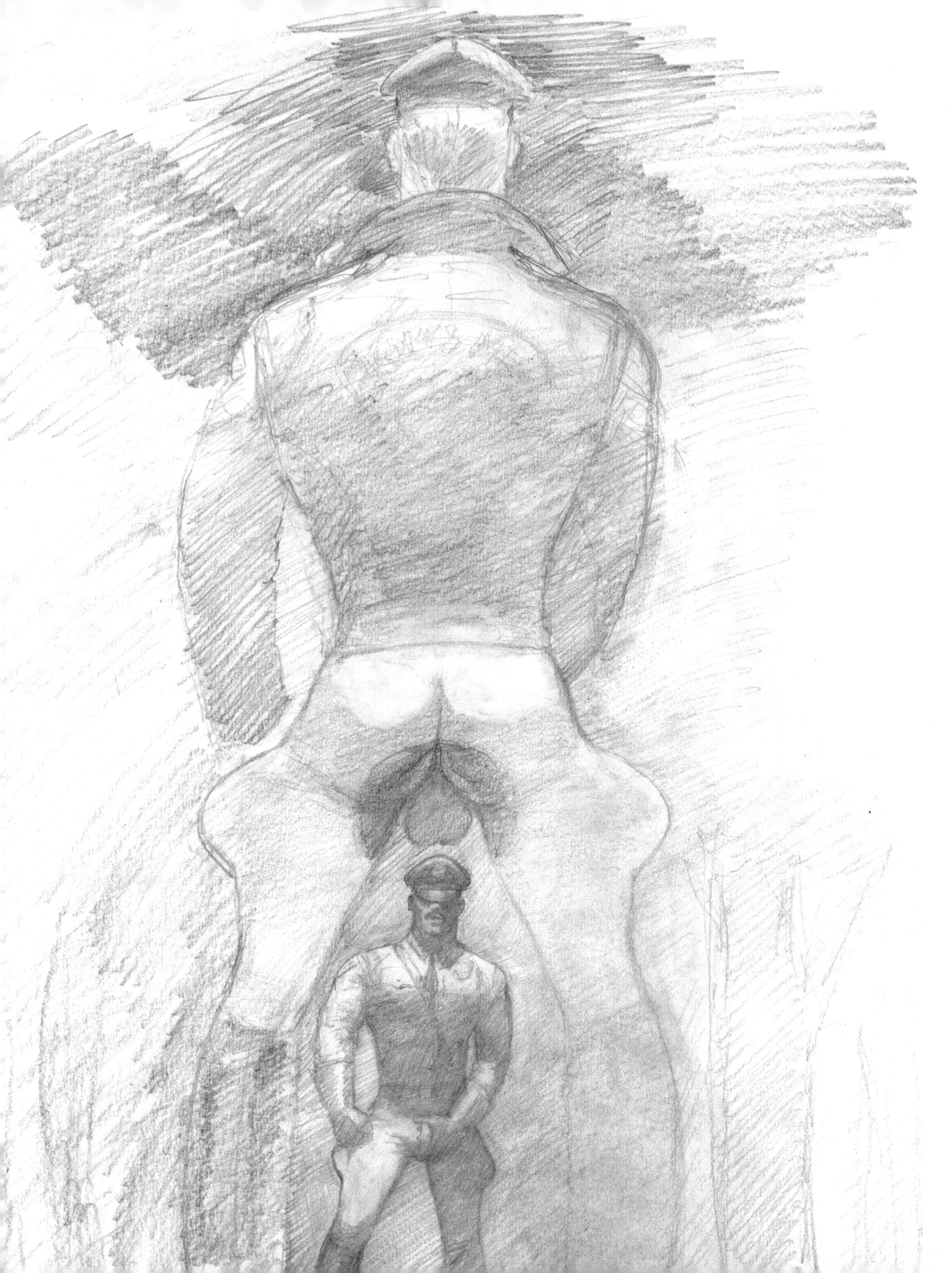

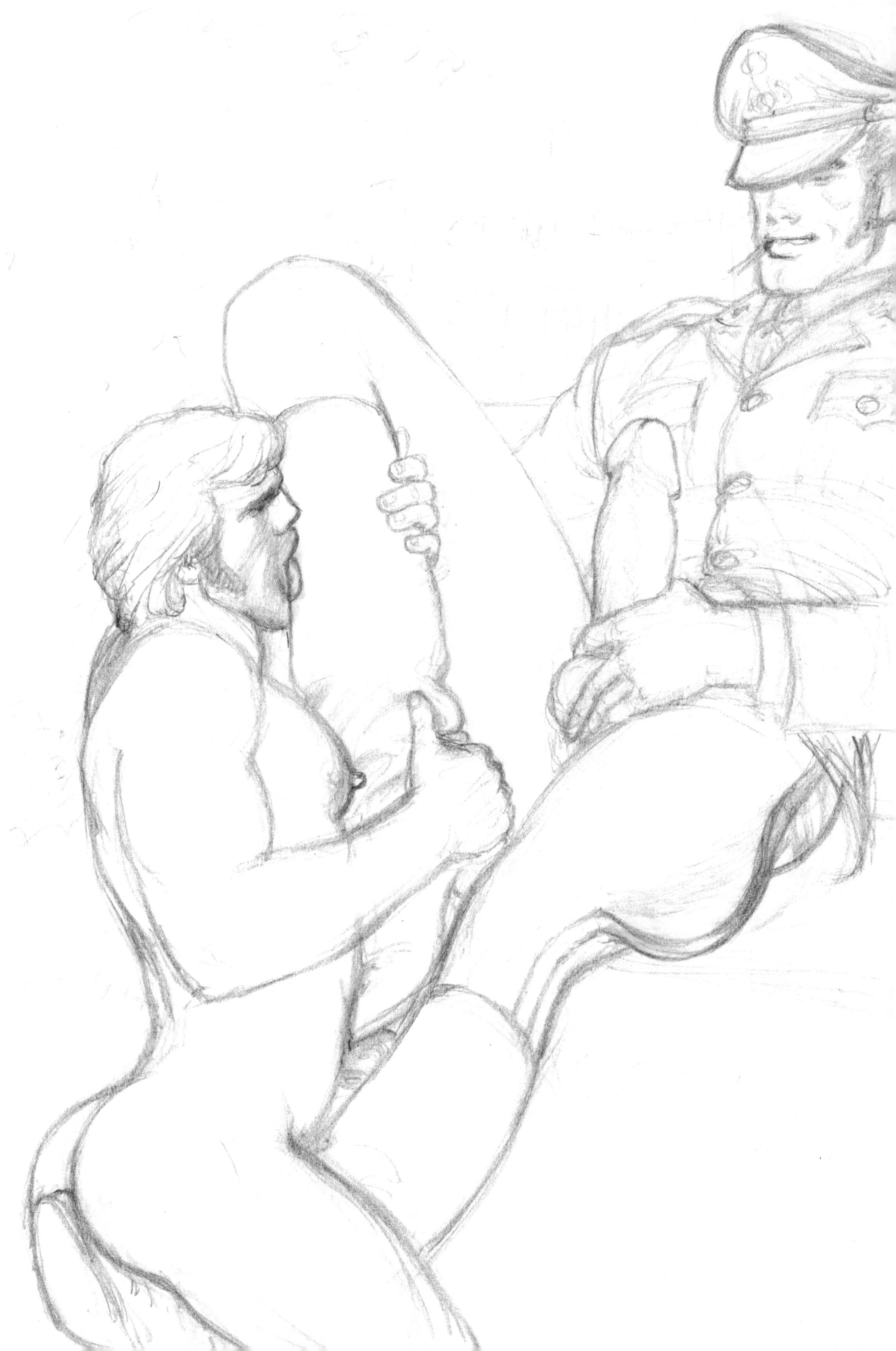

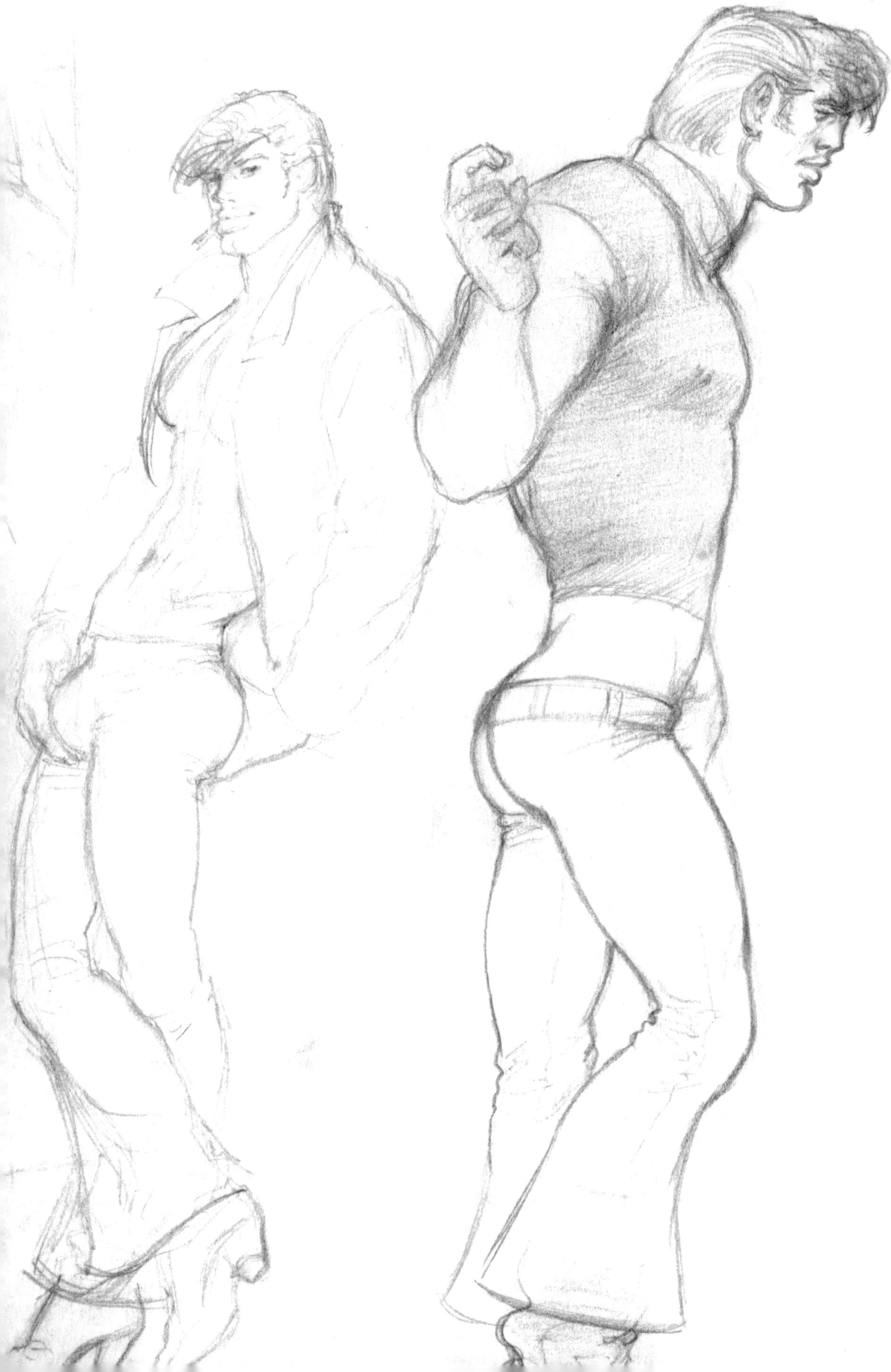

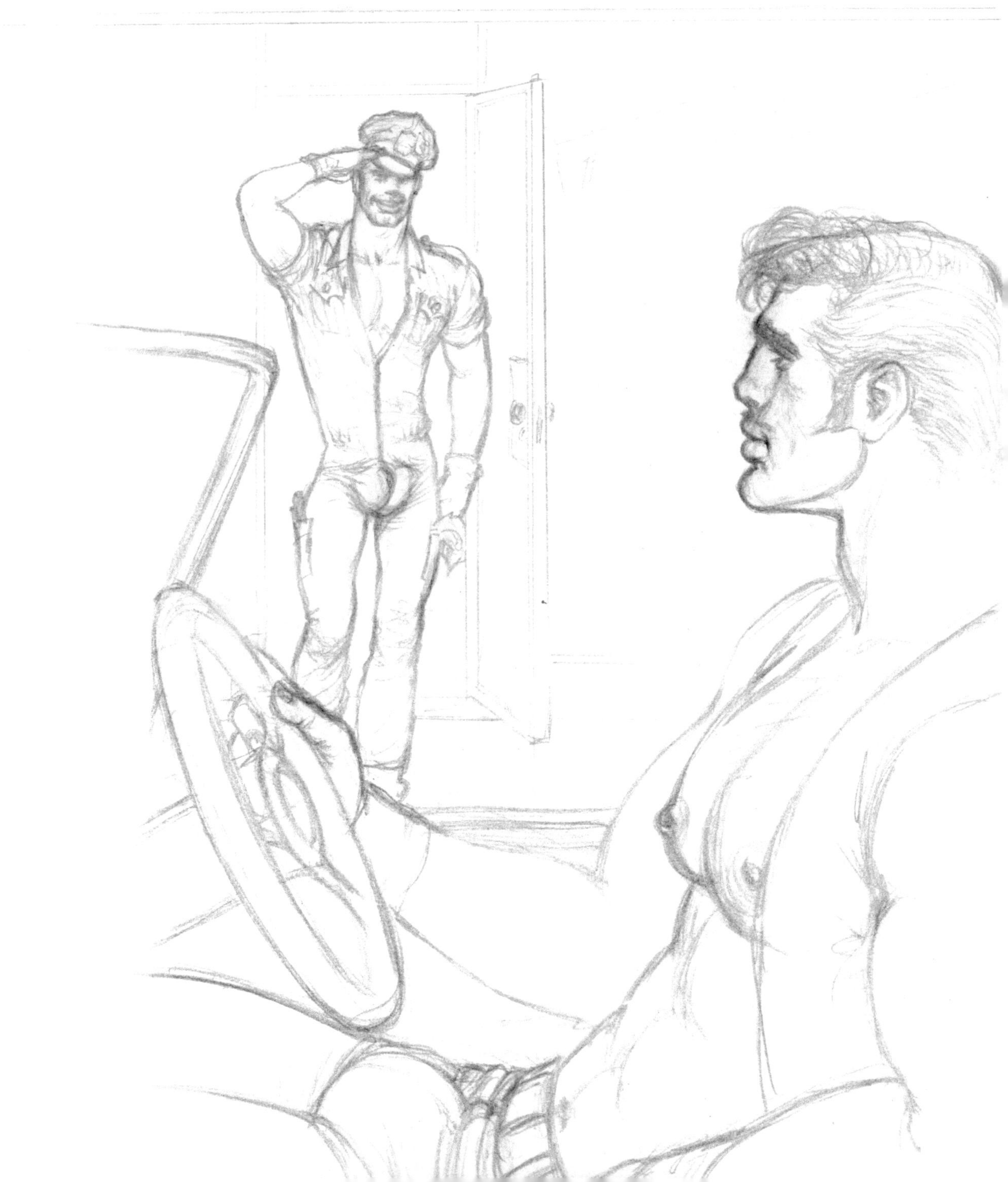

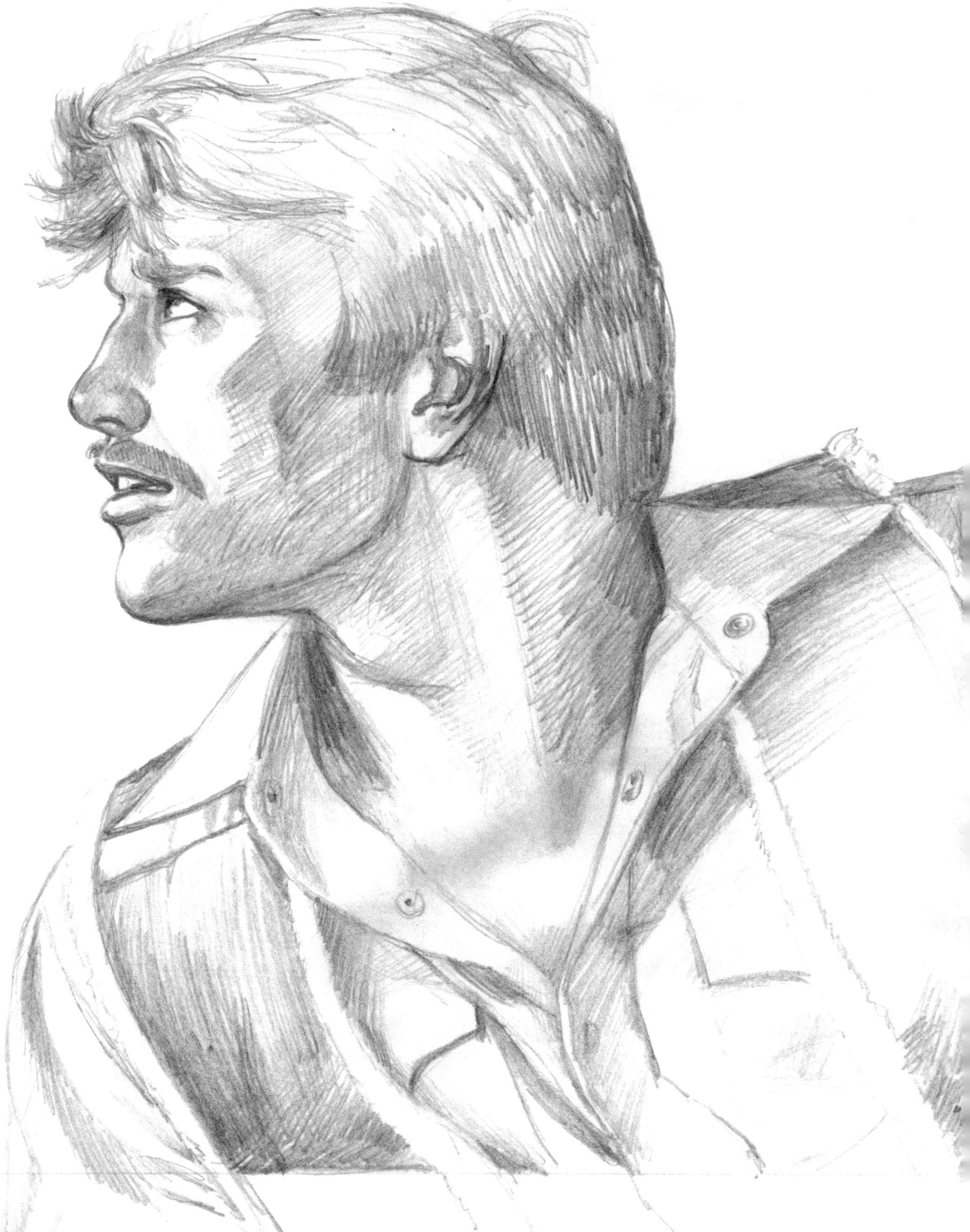

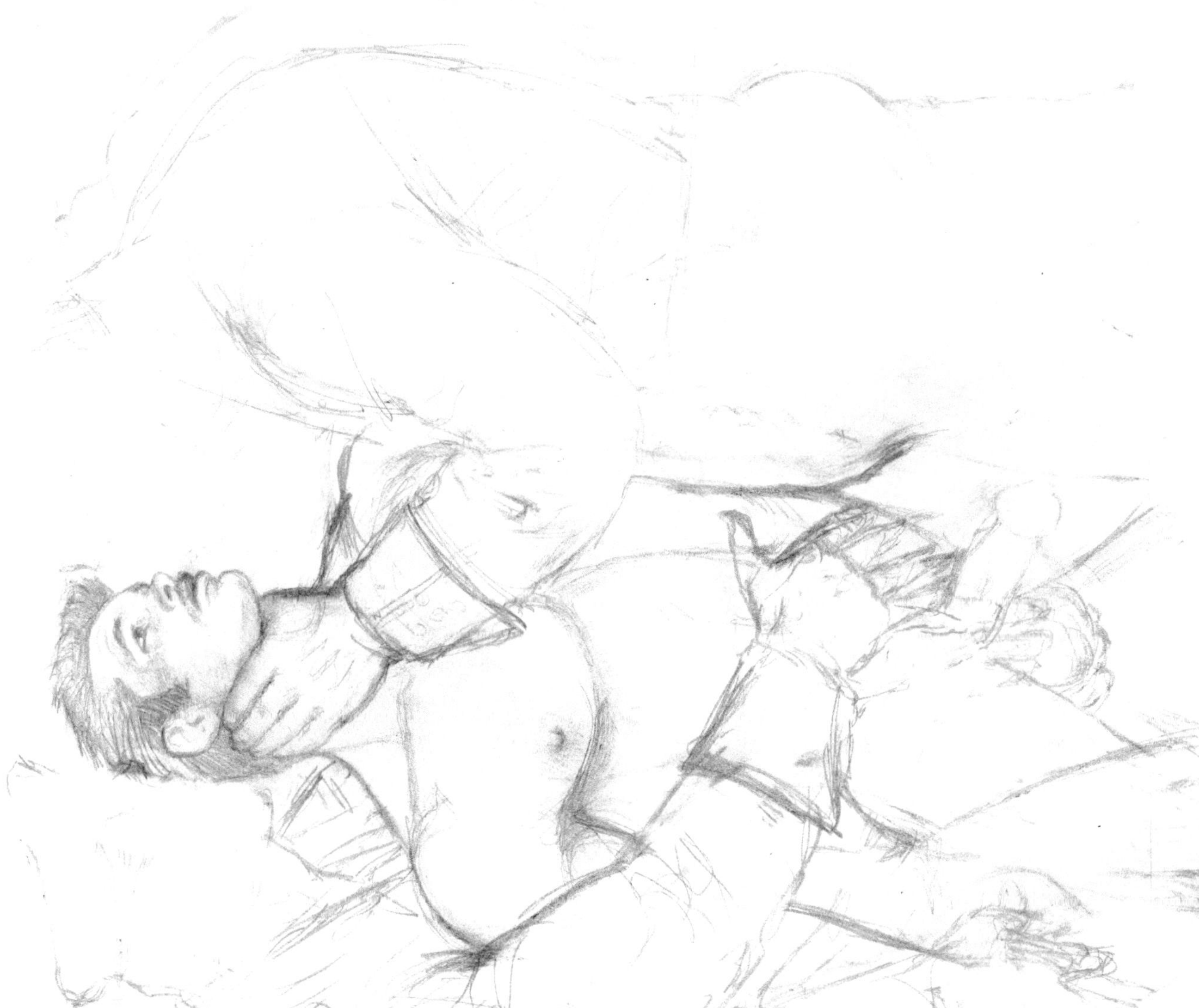

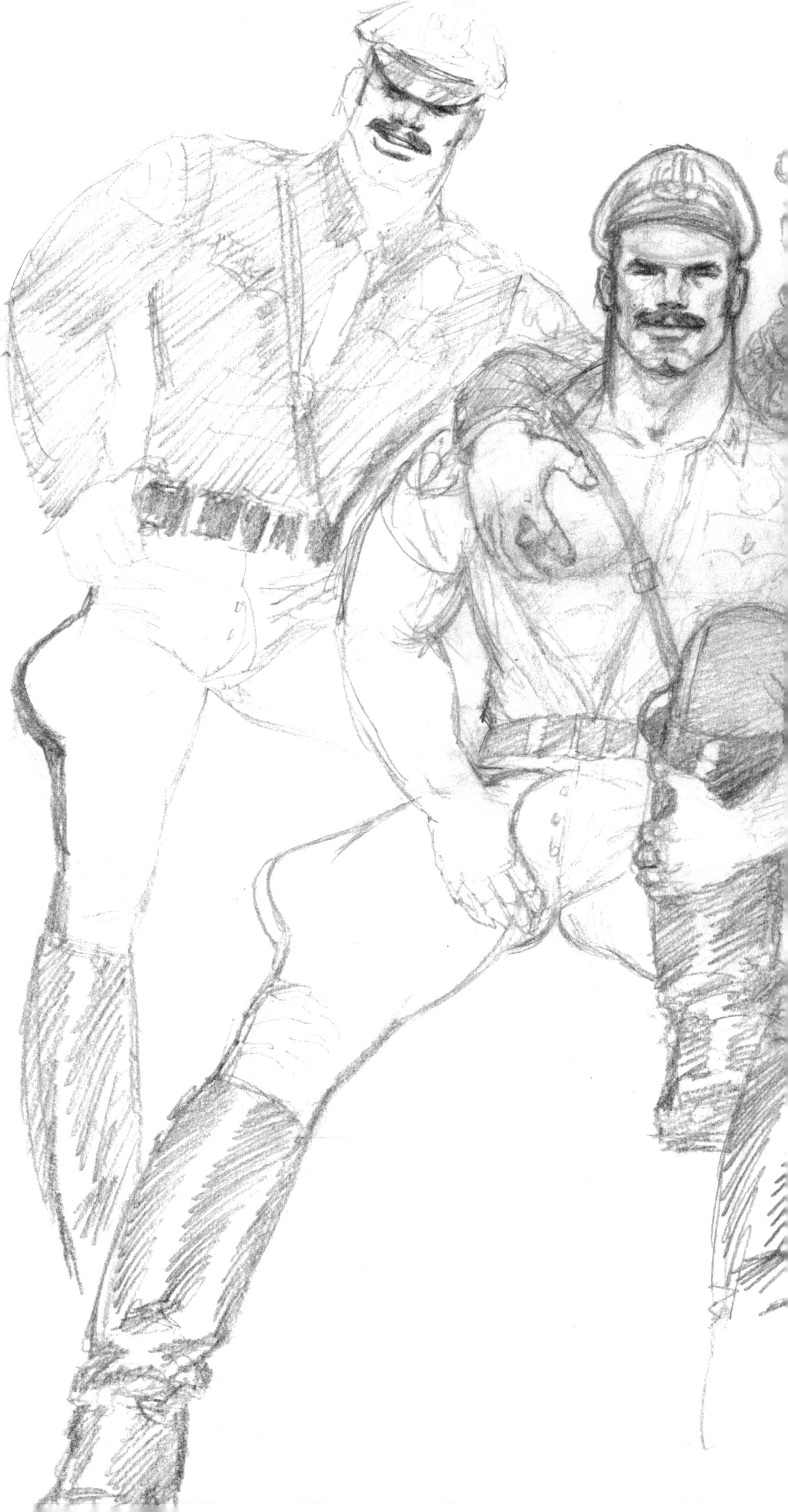

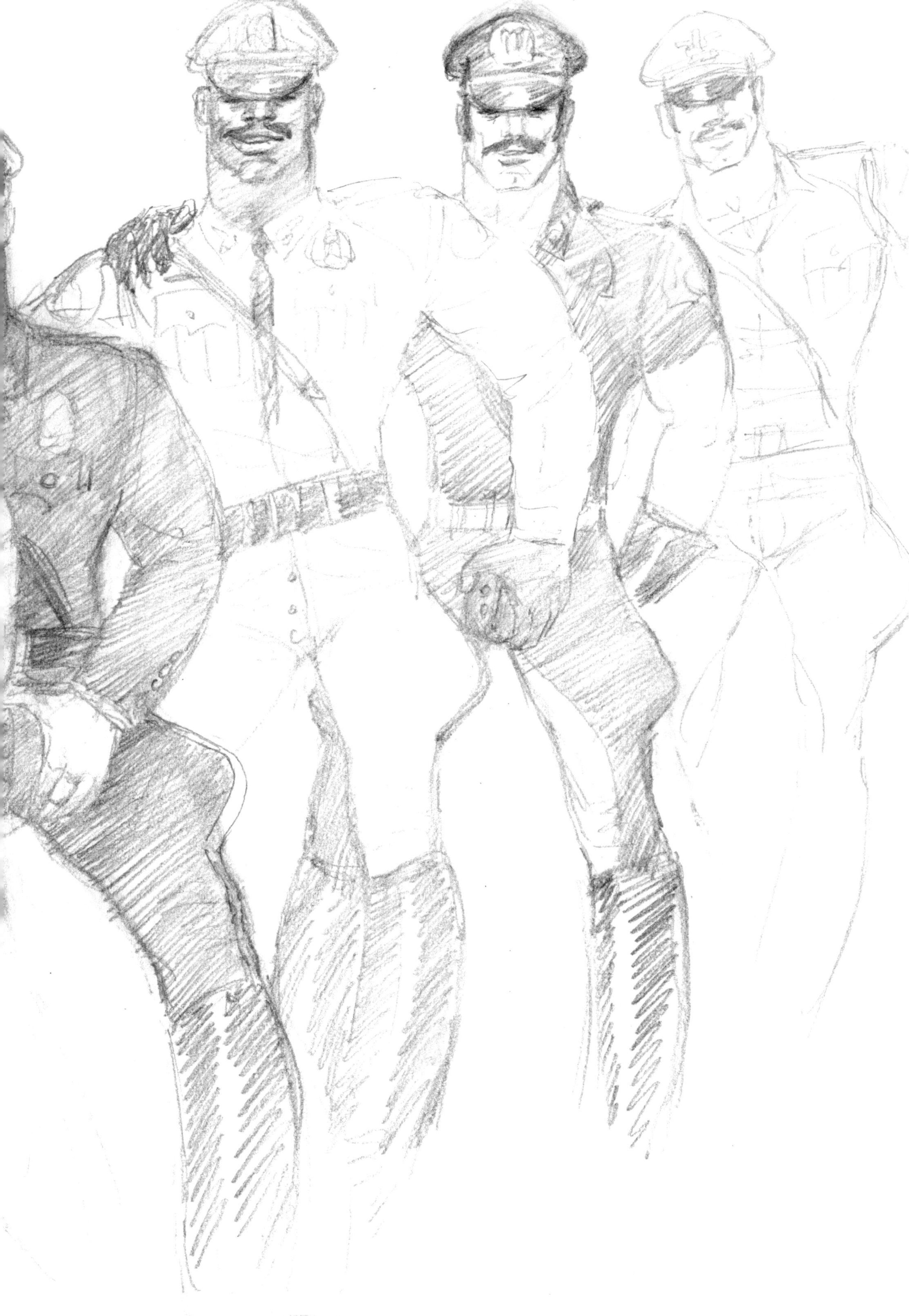

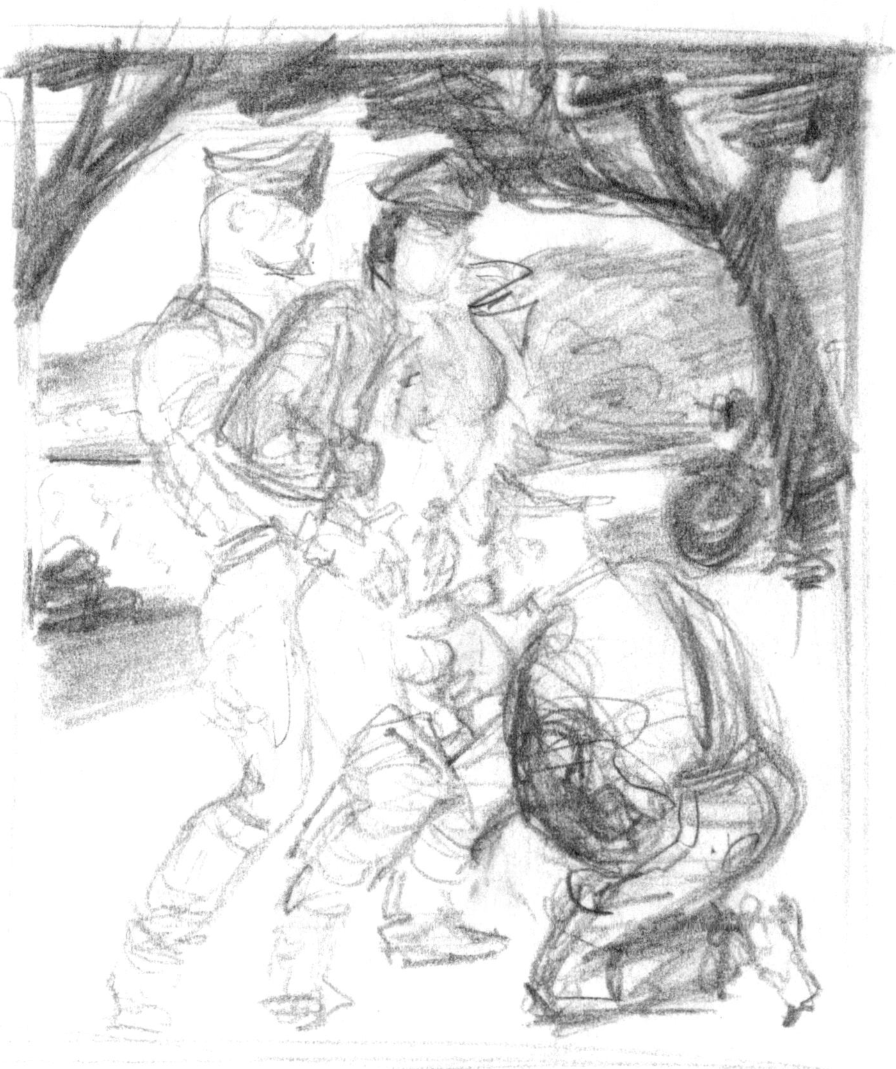

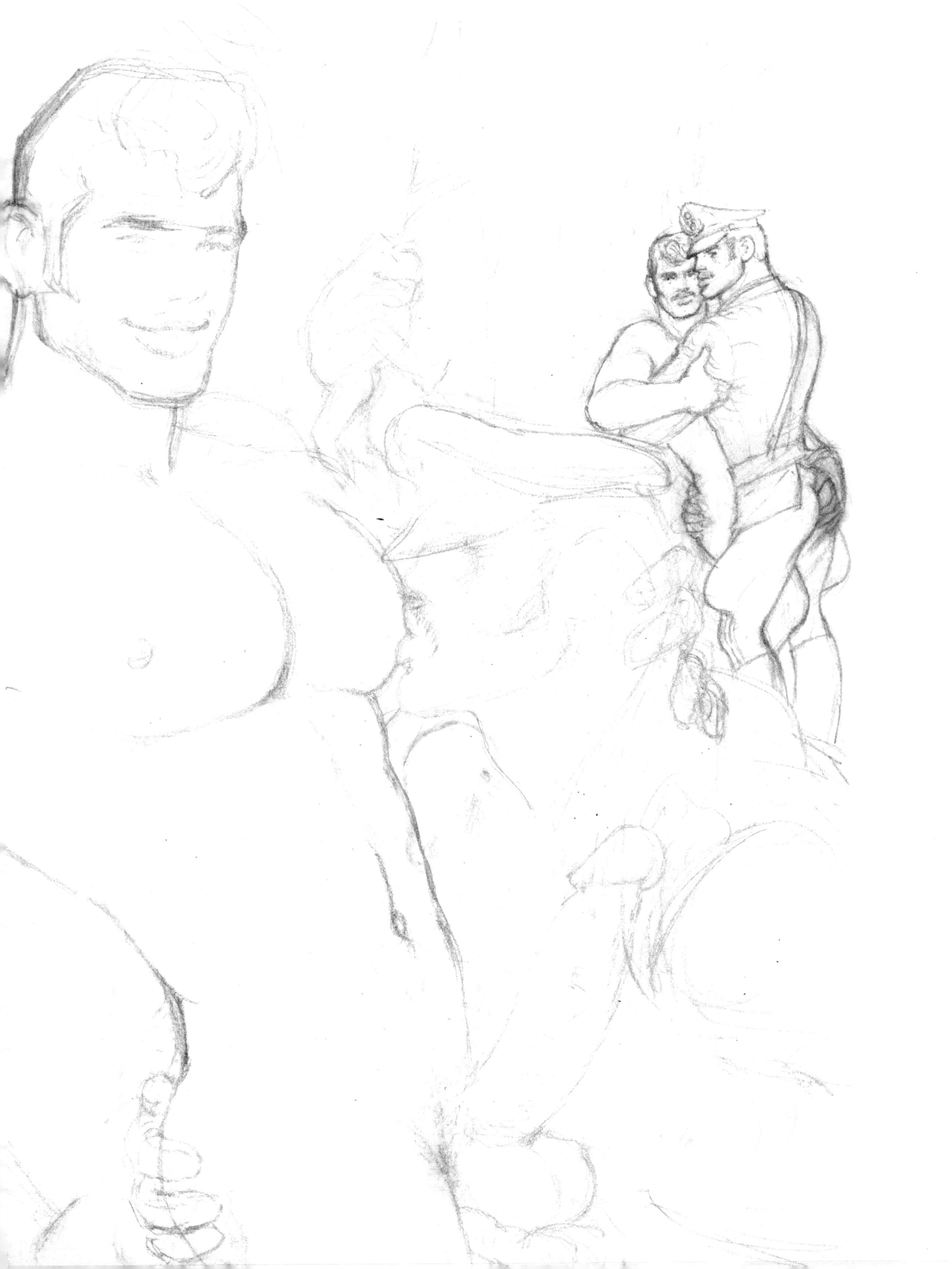

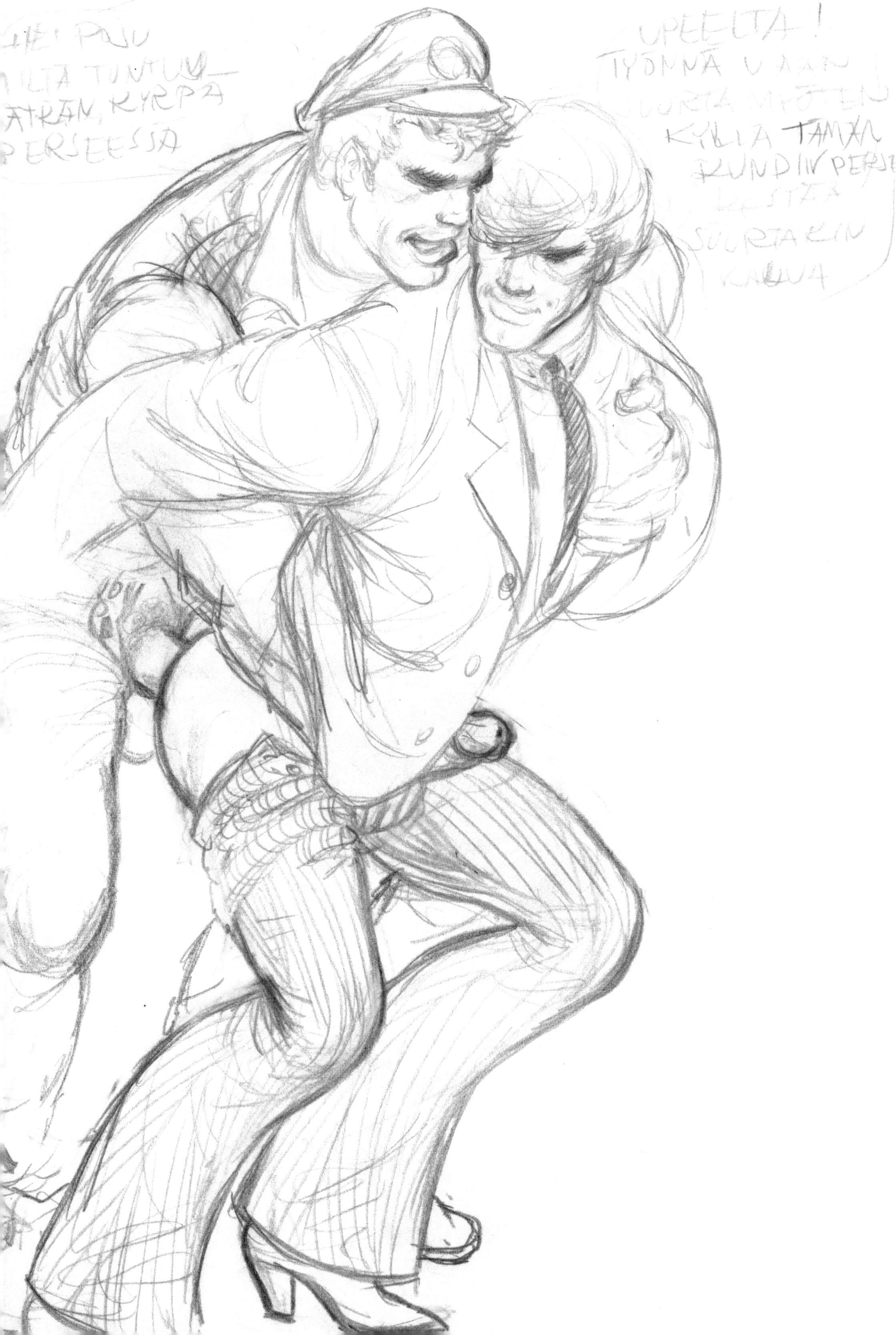
HEI POJU
ILTA TUNTUU
ATRAN, KYRPÄ
PERSEESSÄ
UPEELTA!
TYÖNNÄ VAAN
SUURTA MYÖTEN
KYLLÄ TÄMÄN
RUNDIN PERSE
KESTÄÄ
SUURTAKIN
KALUA

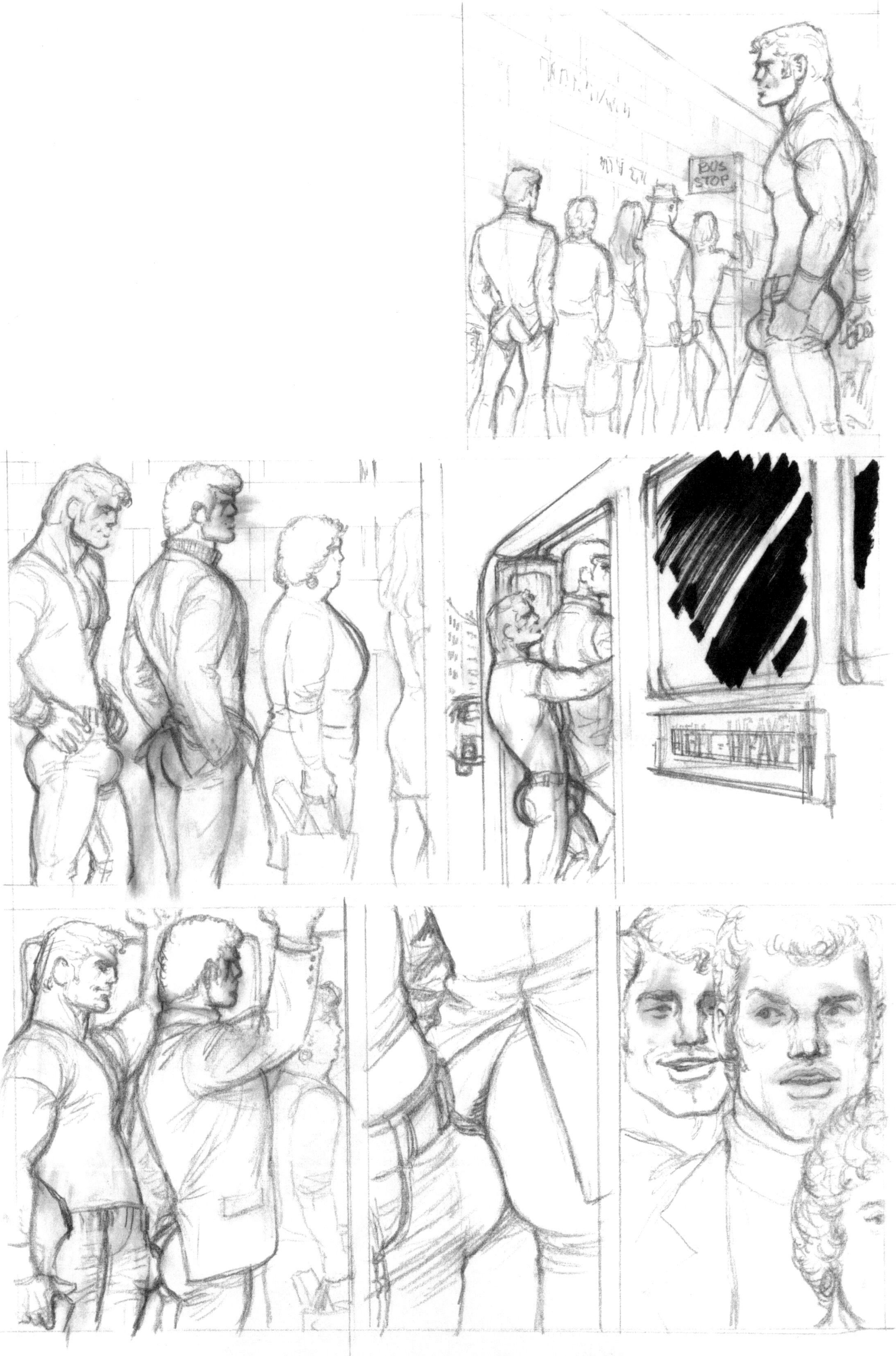
BUS STOP

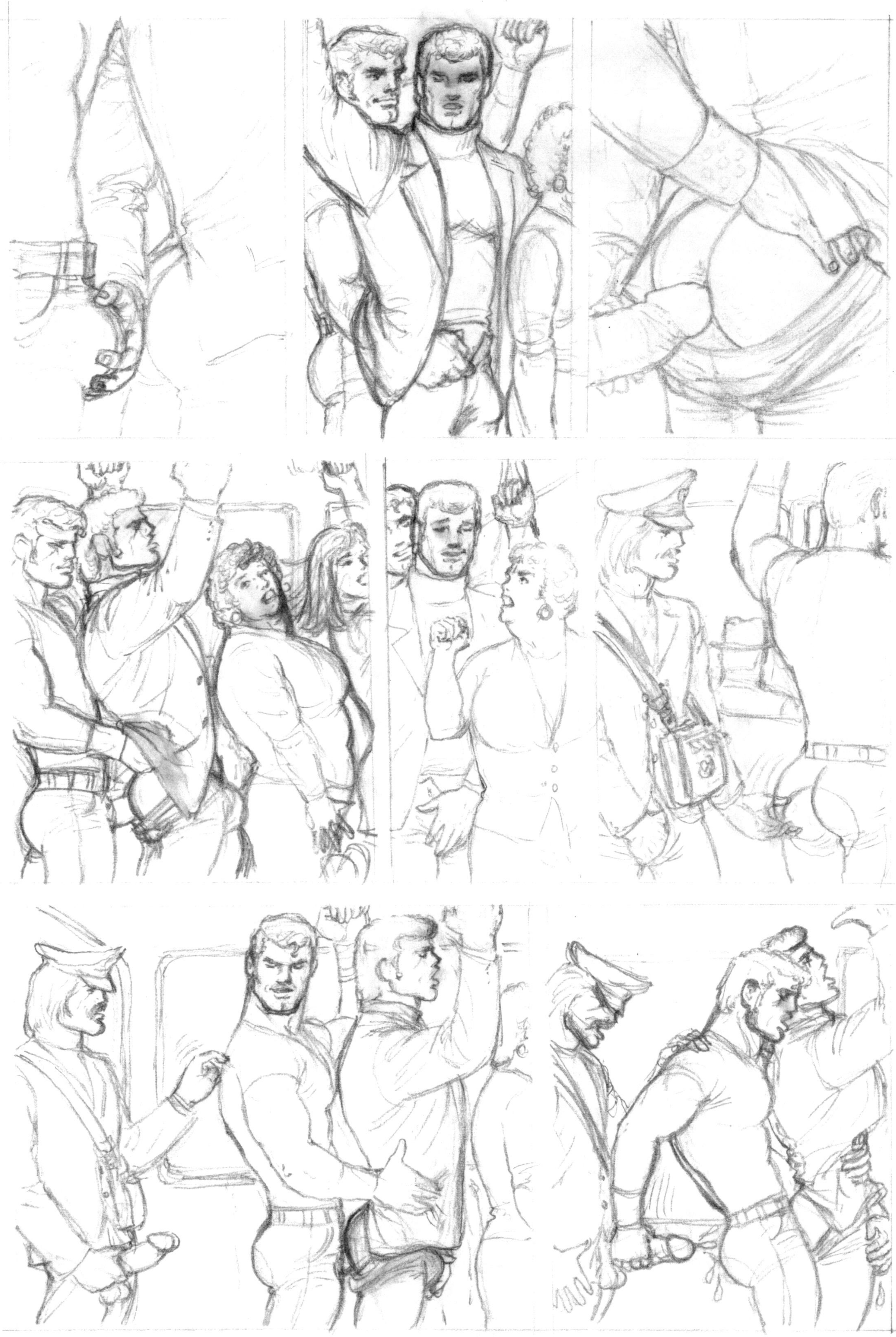

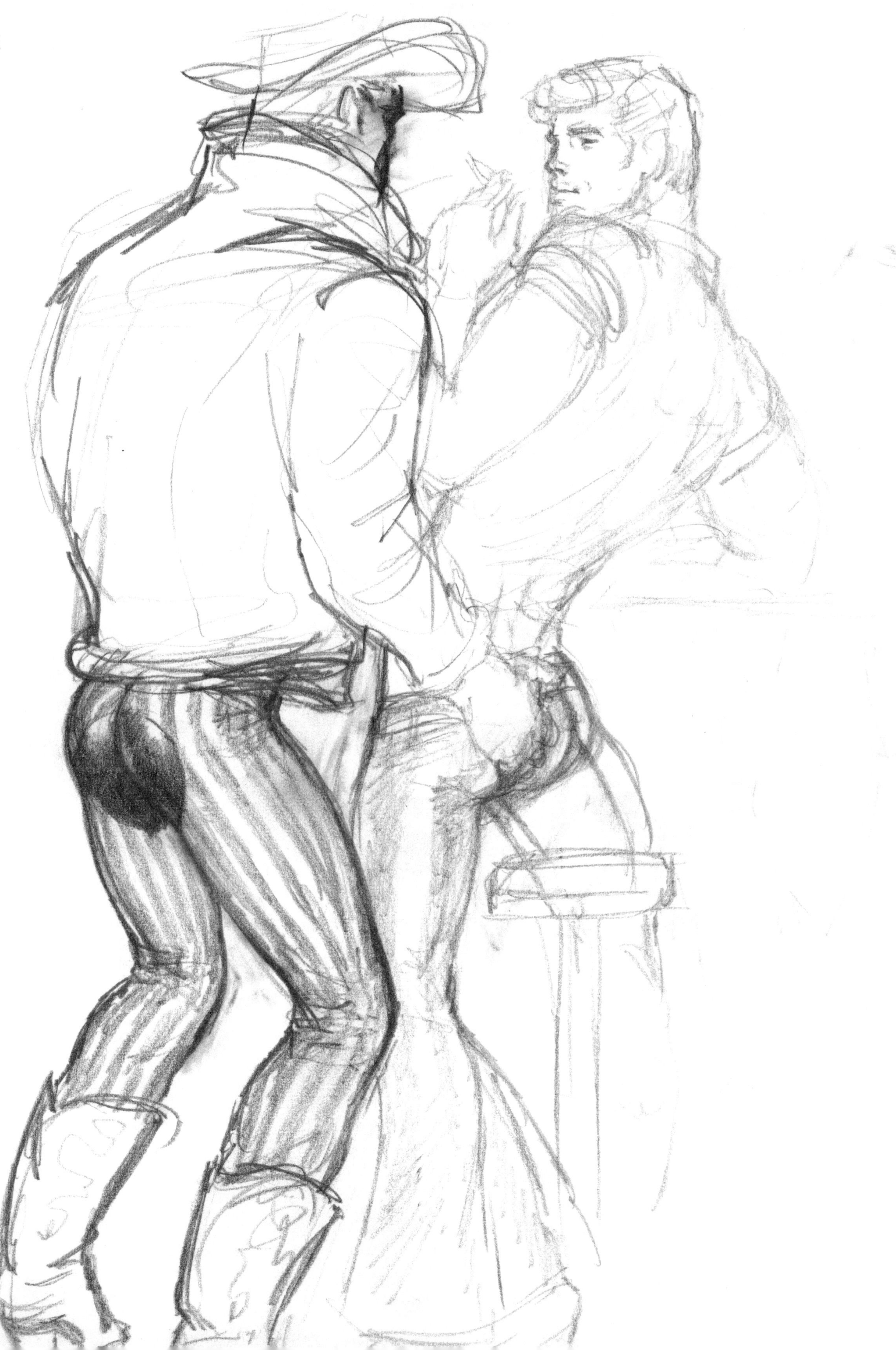

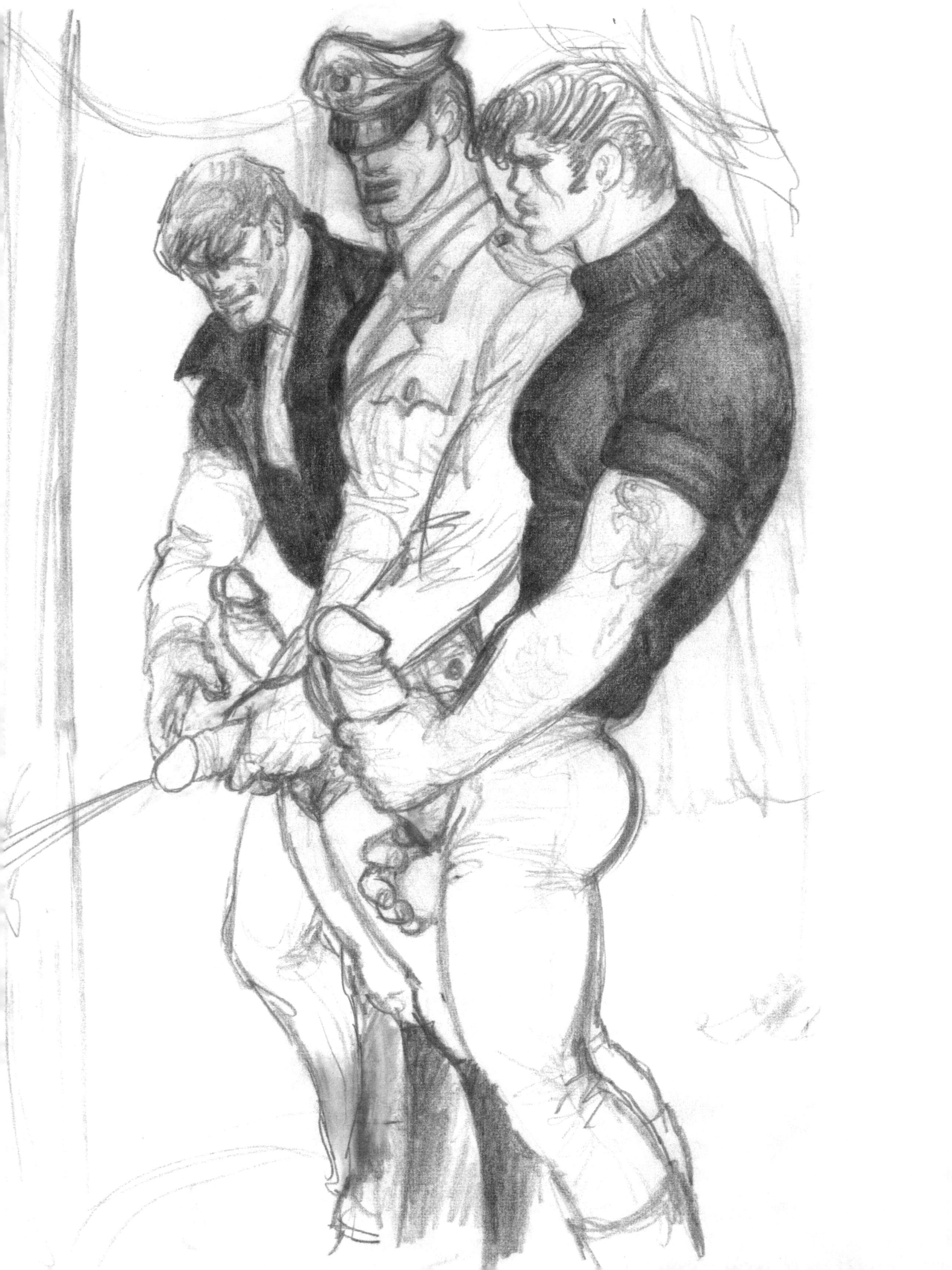

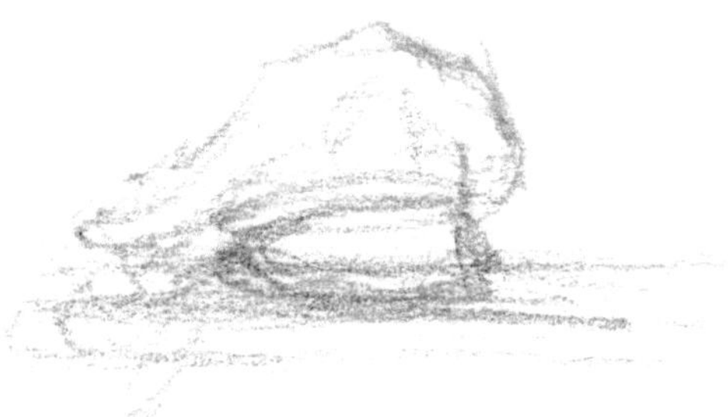

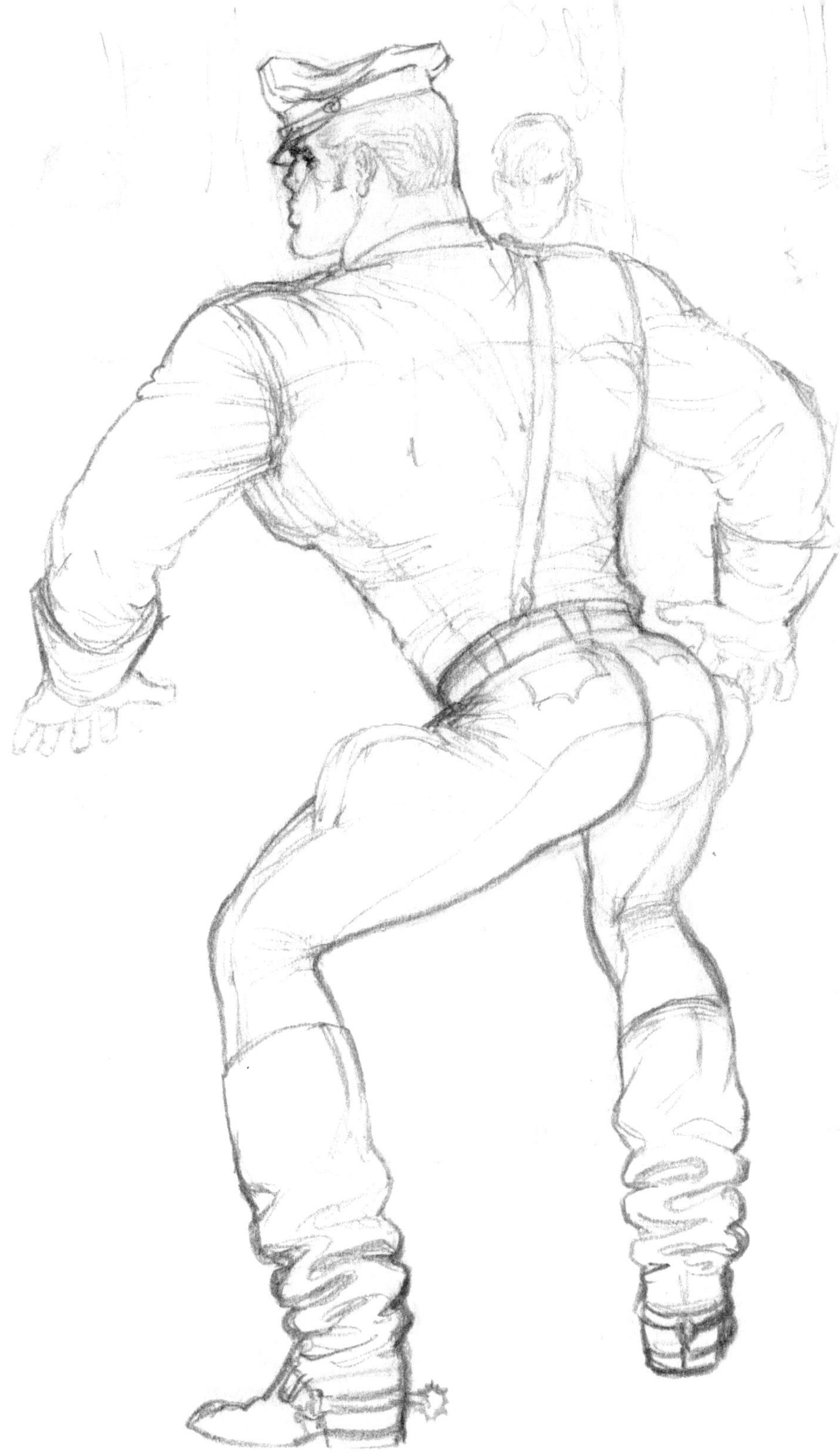

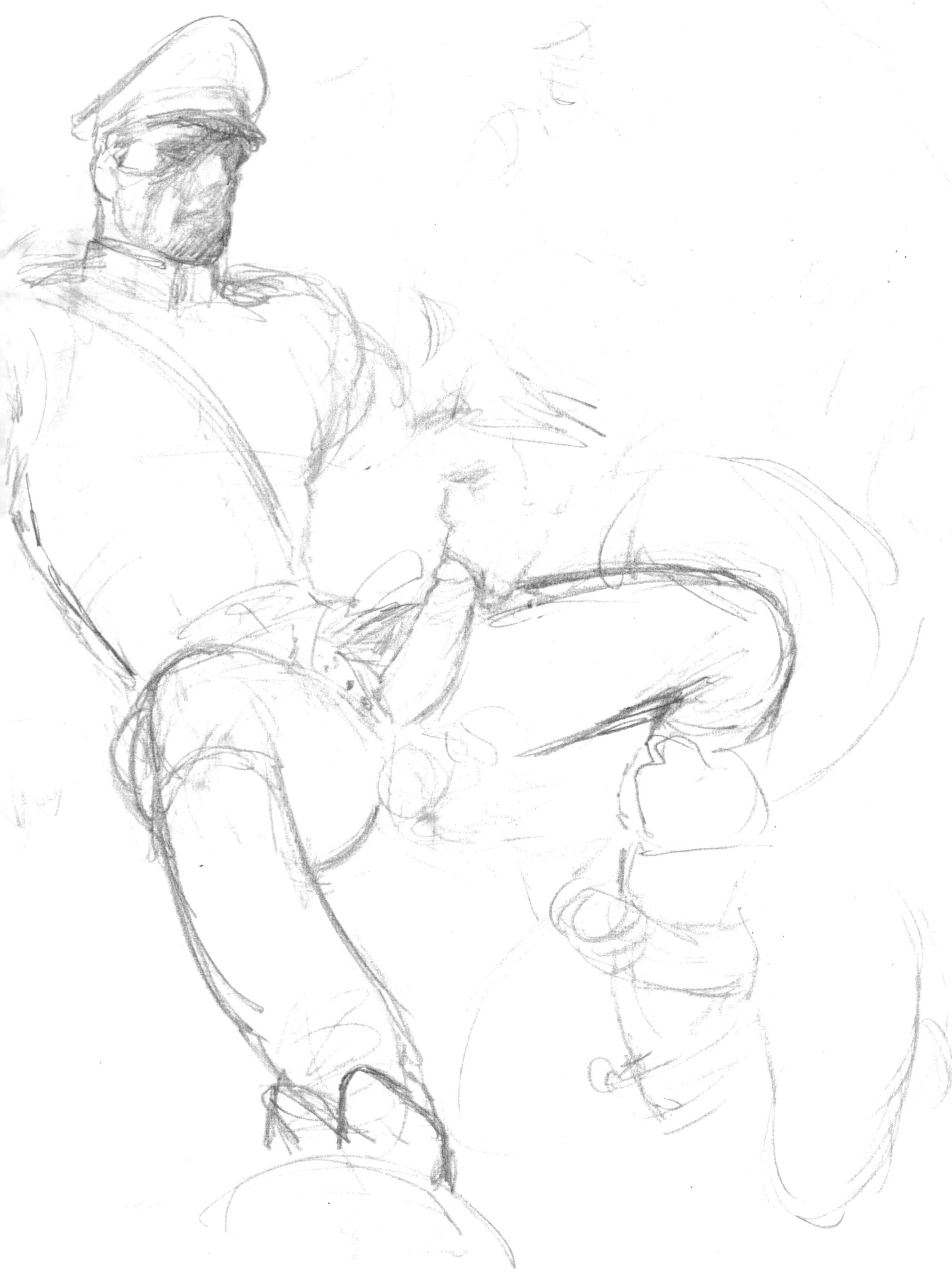

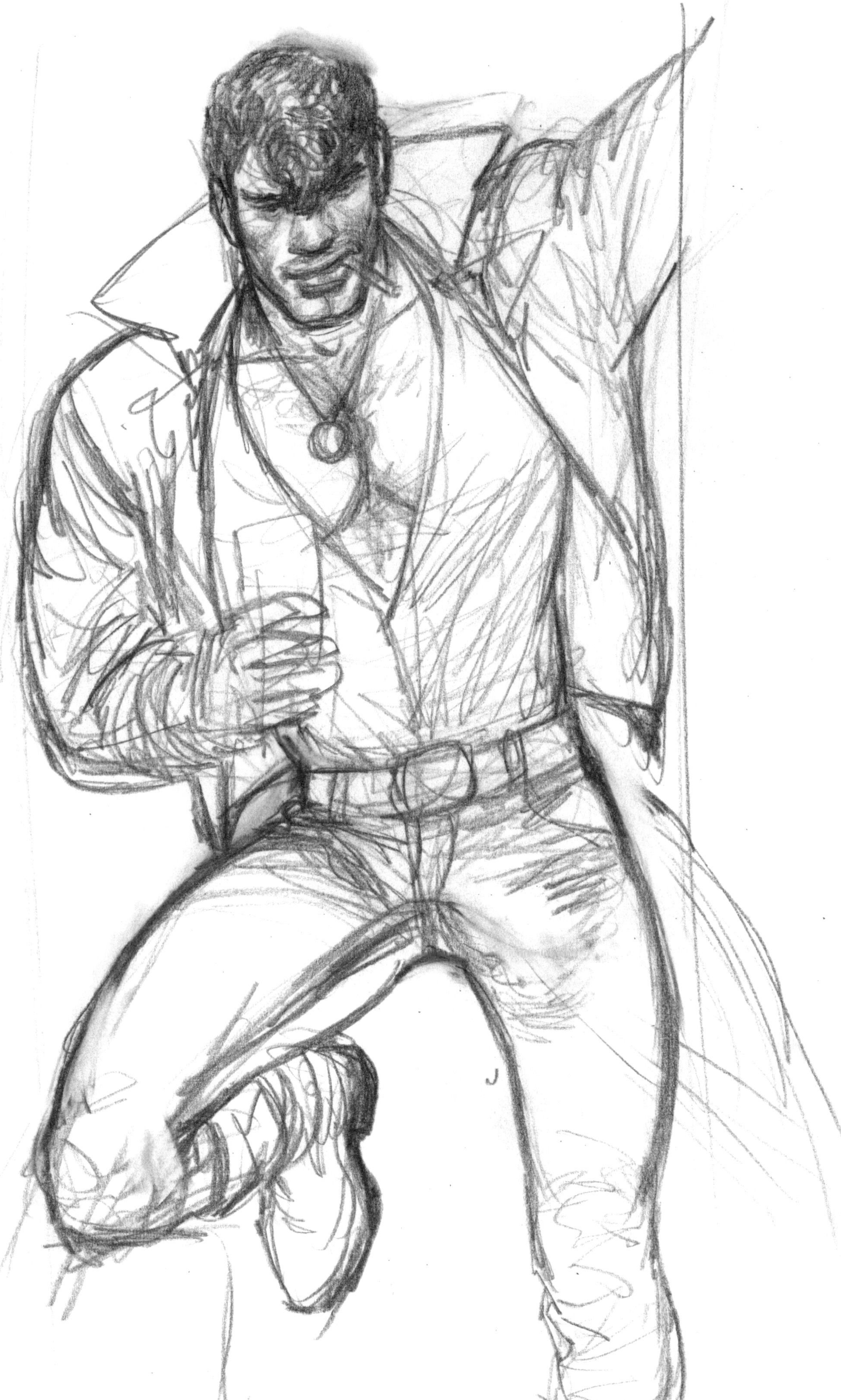

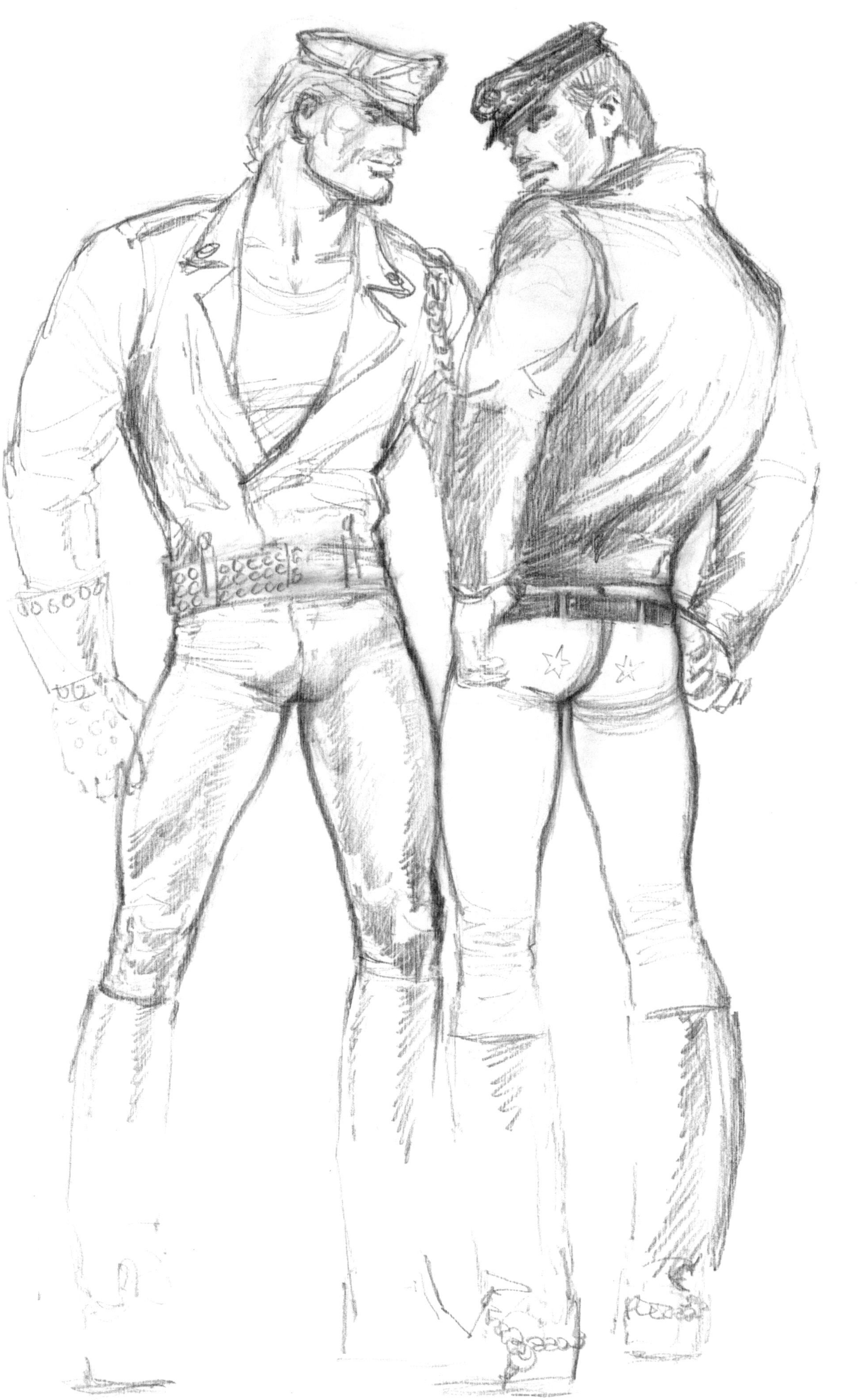

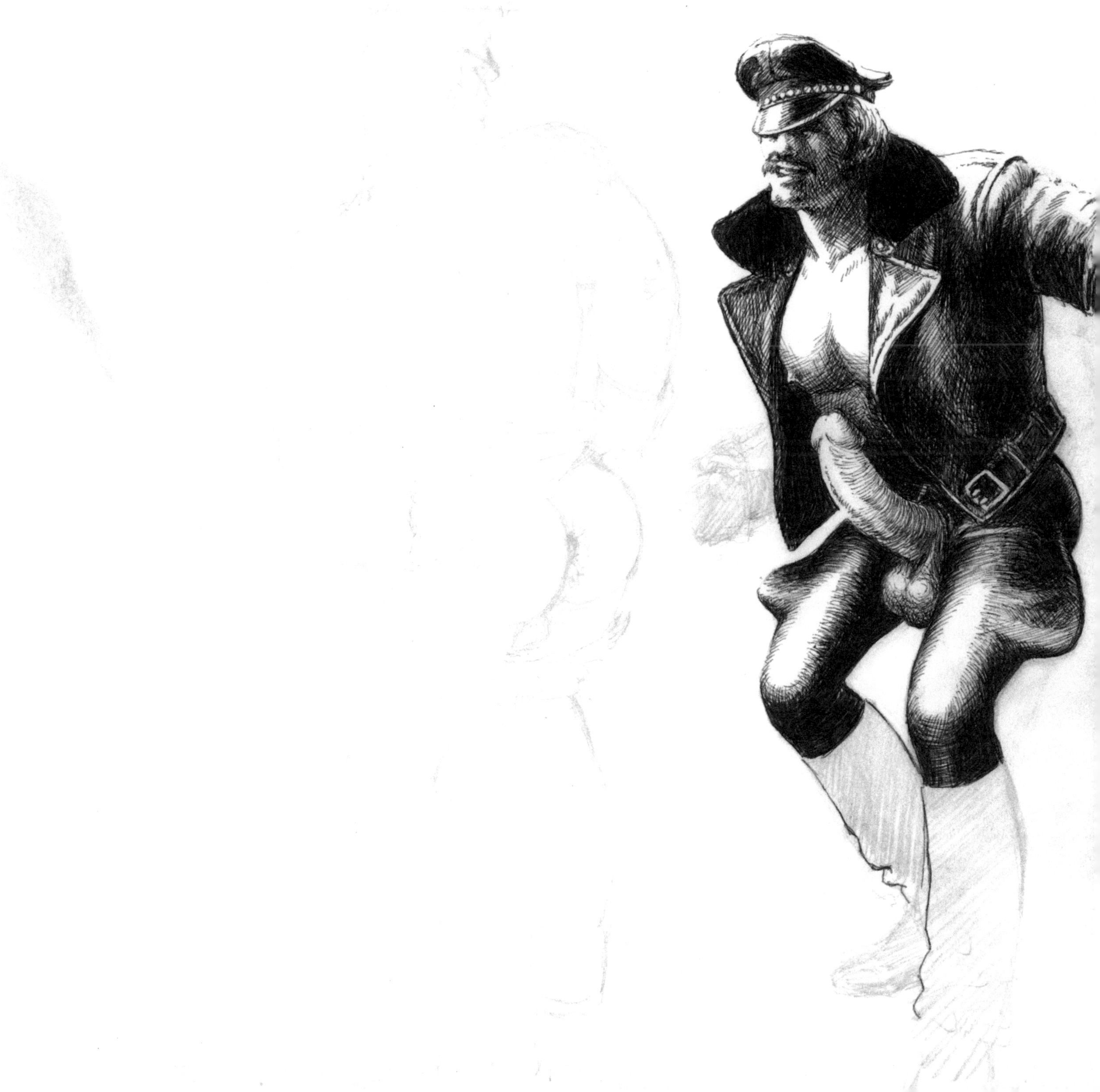

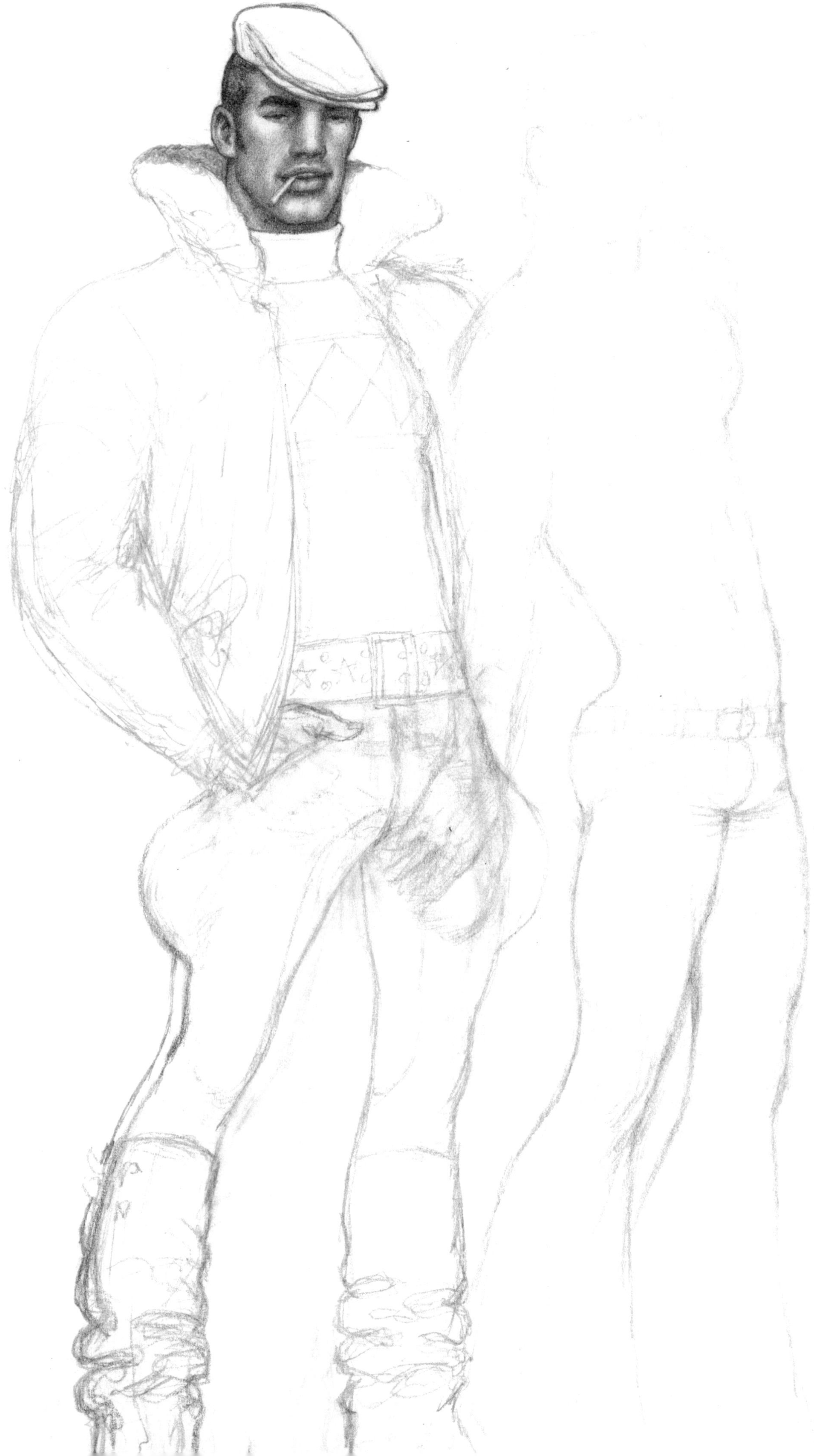

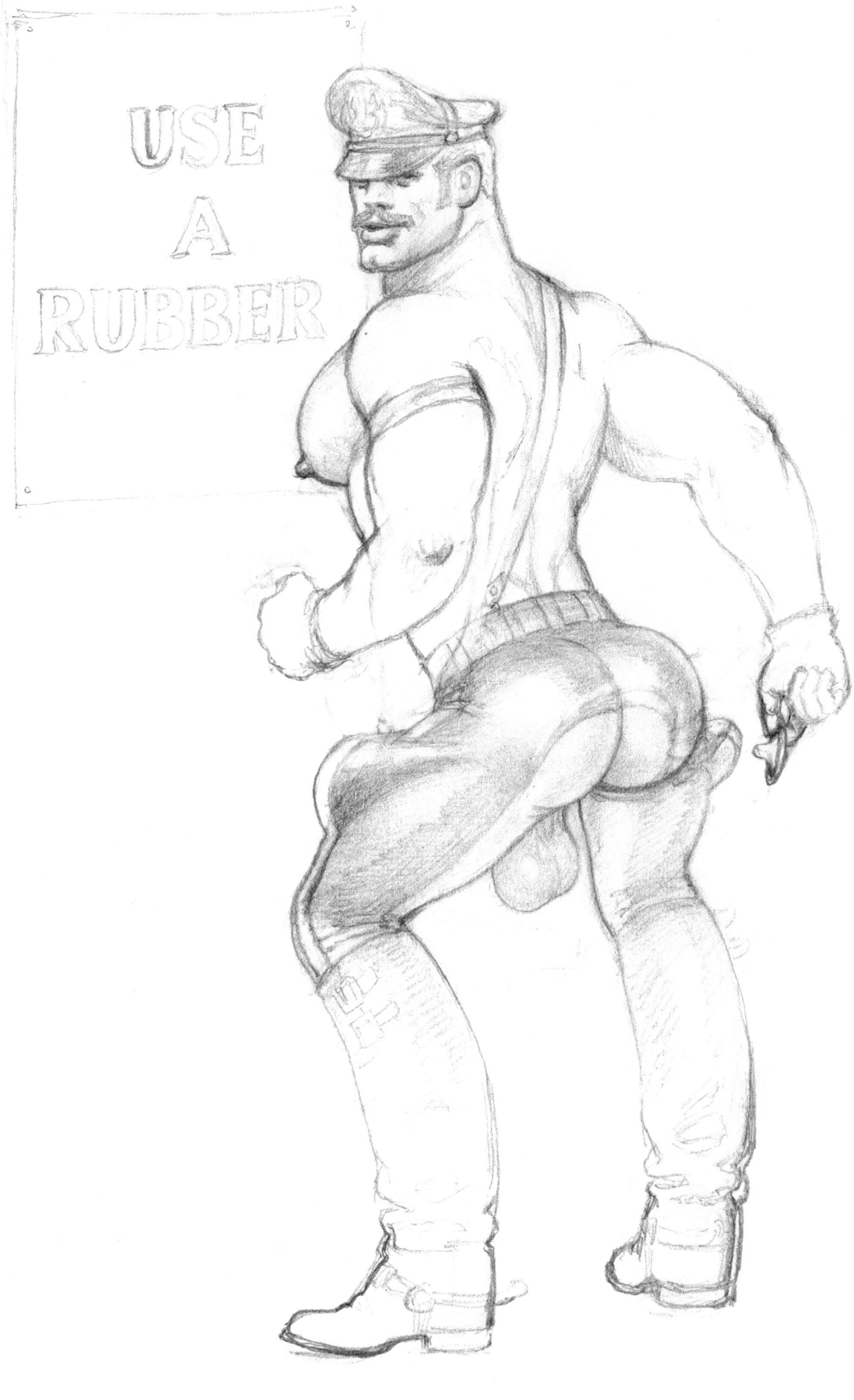
USE
A
RUBBER

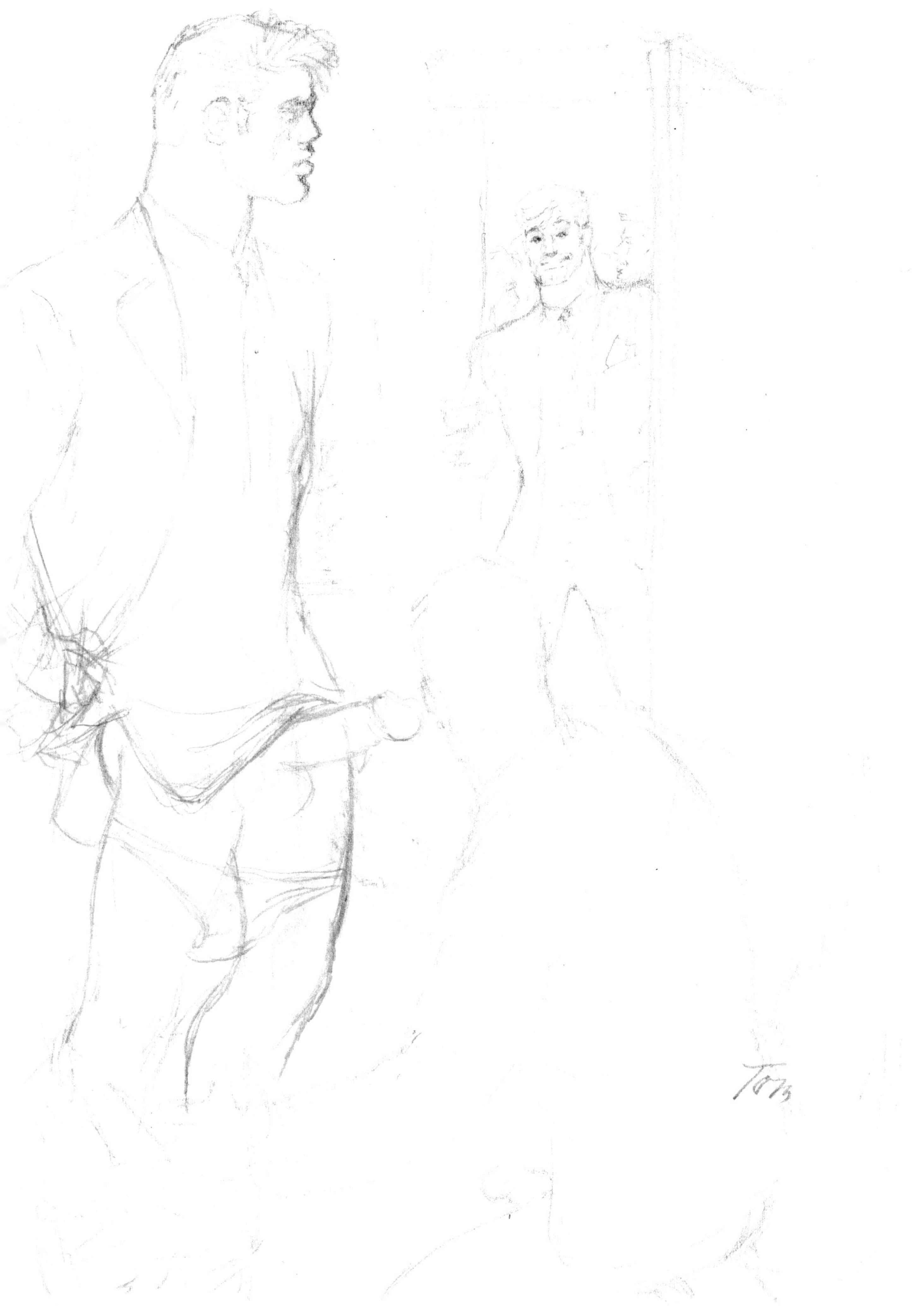
Tom

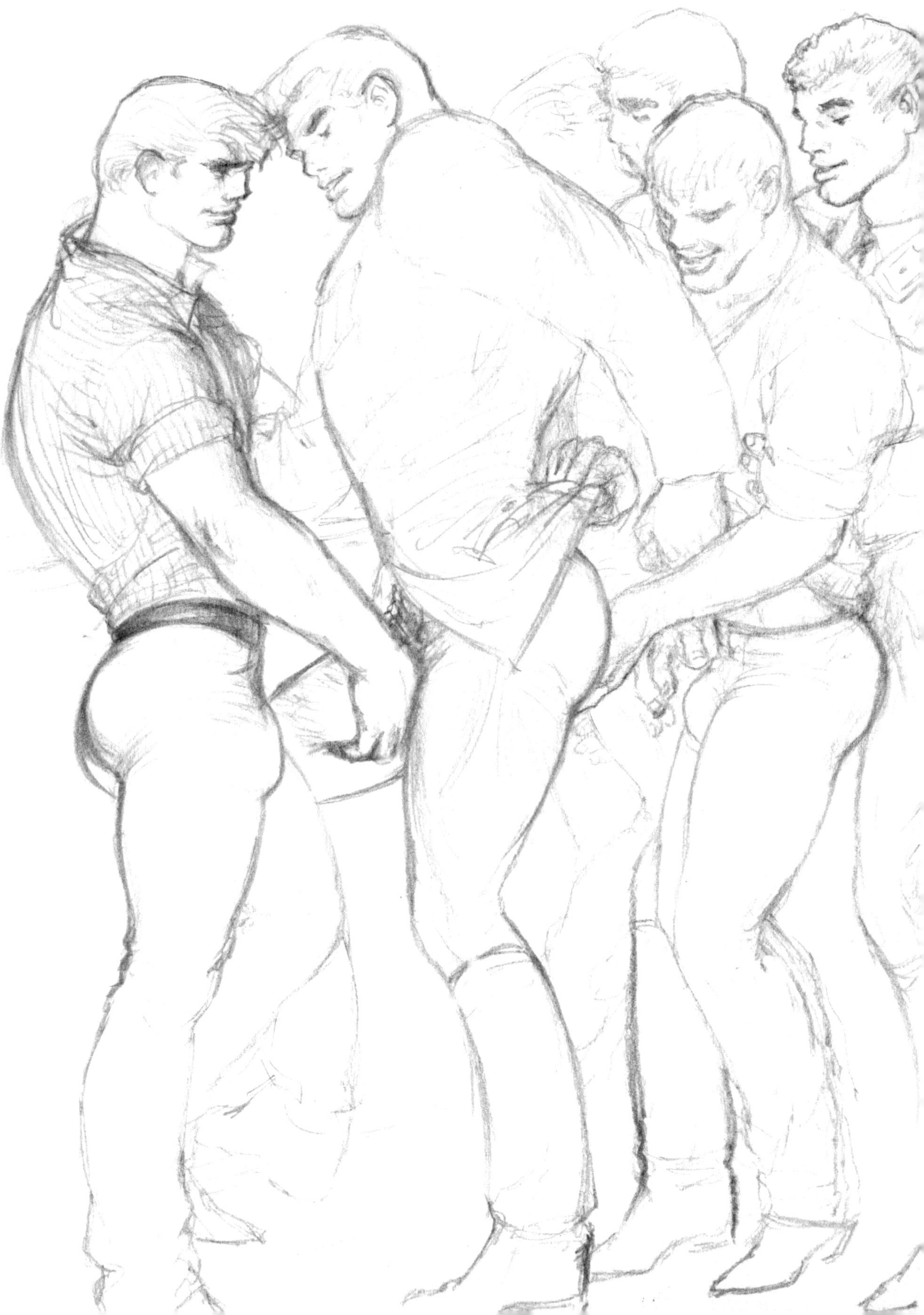

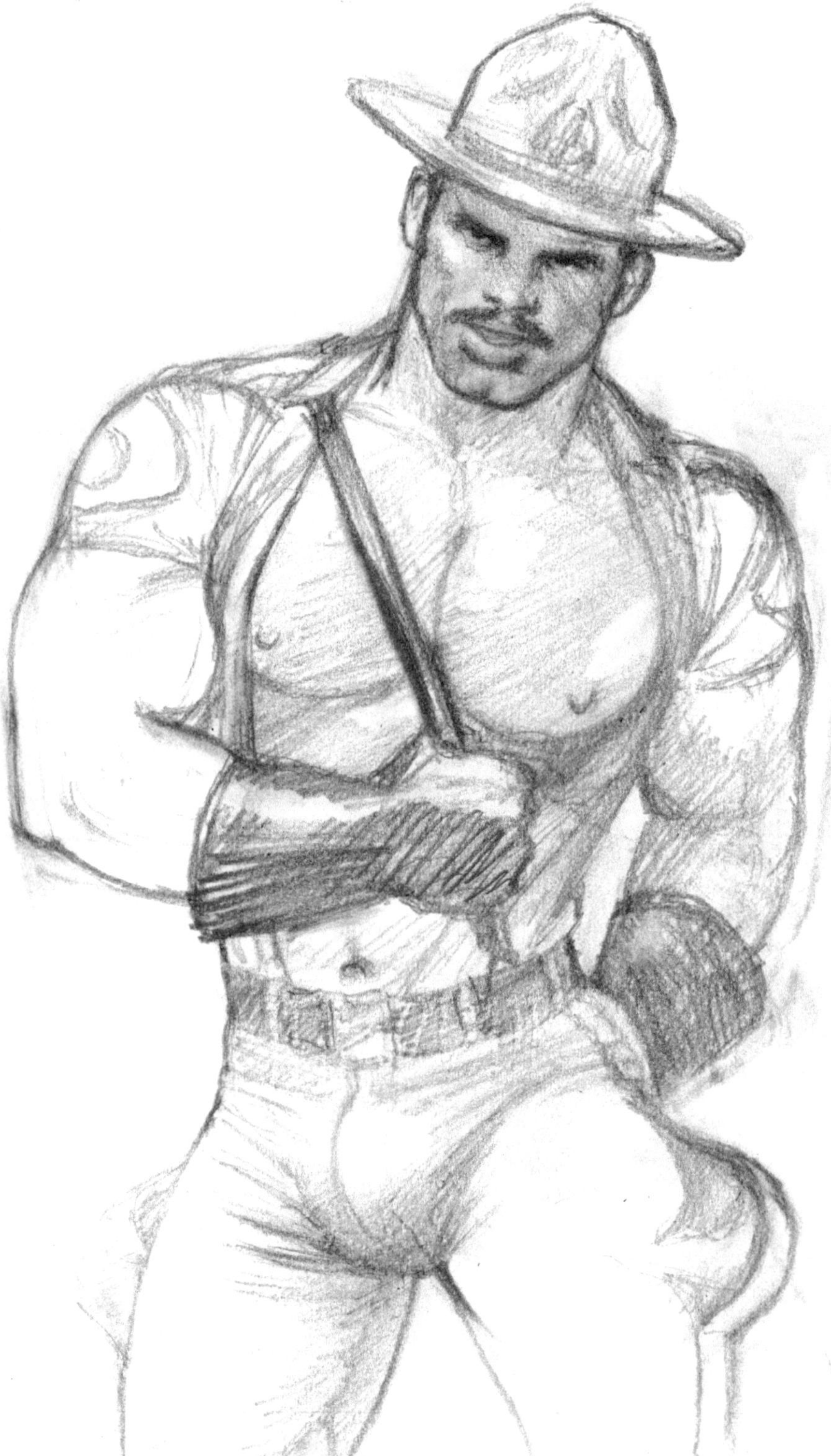

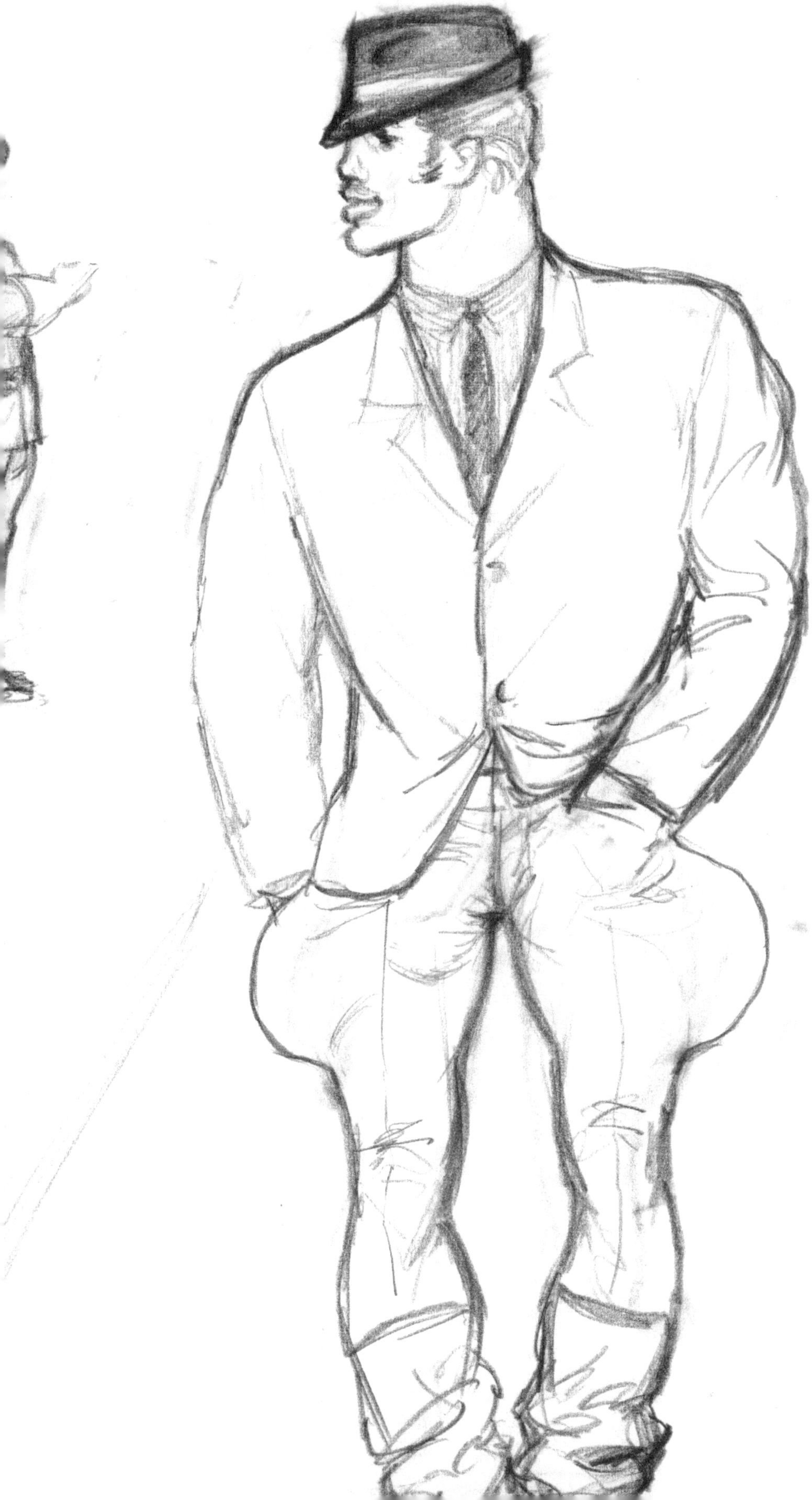

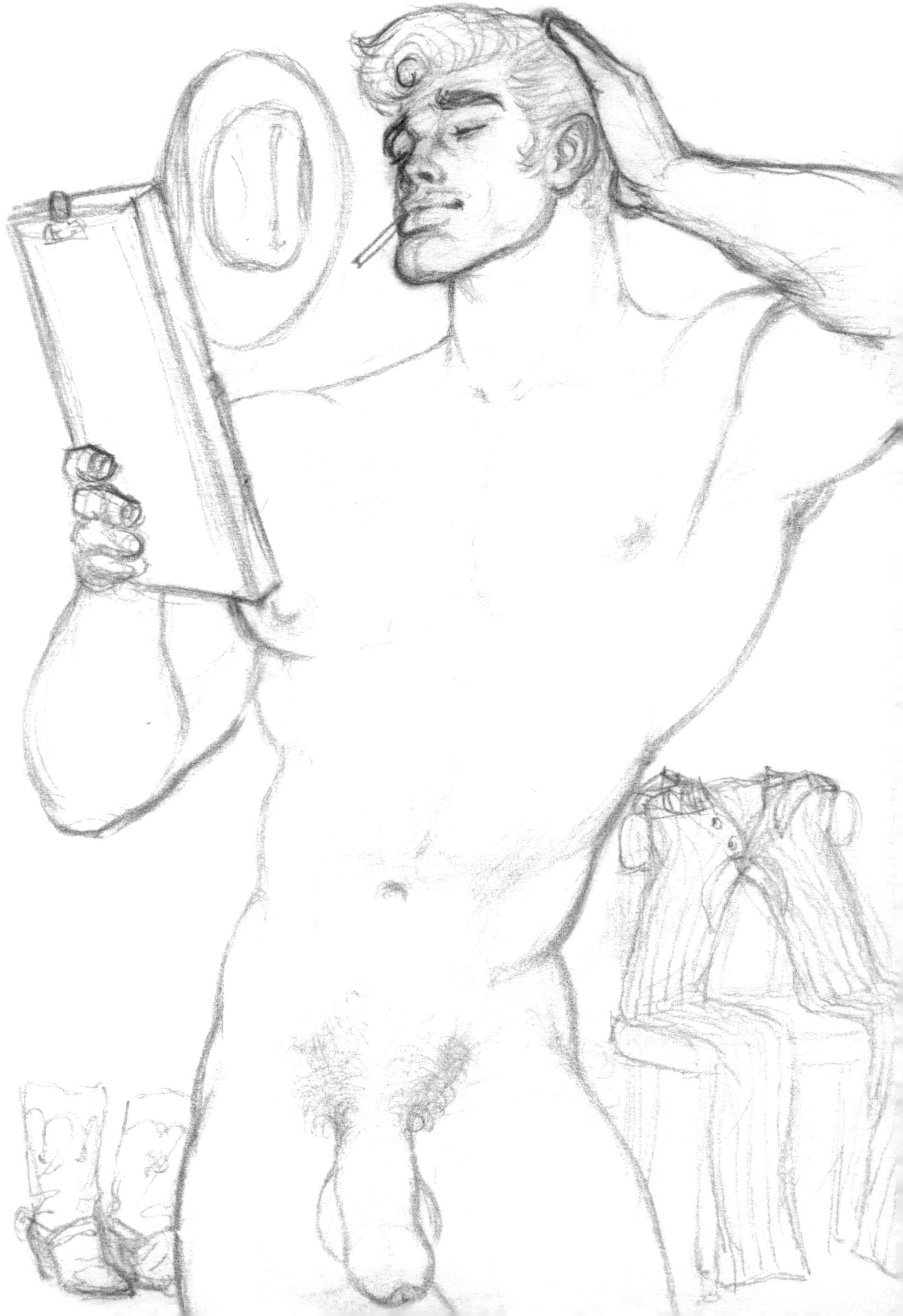

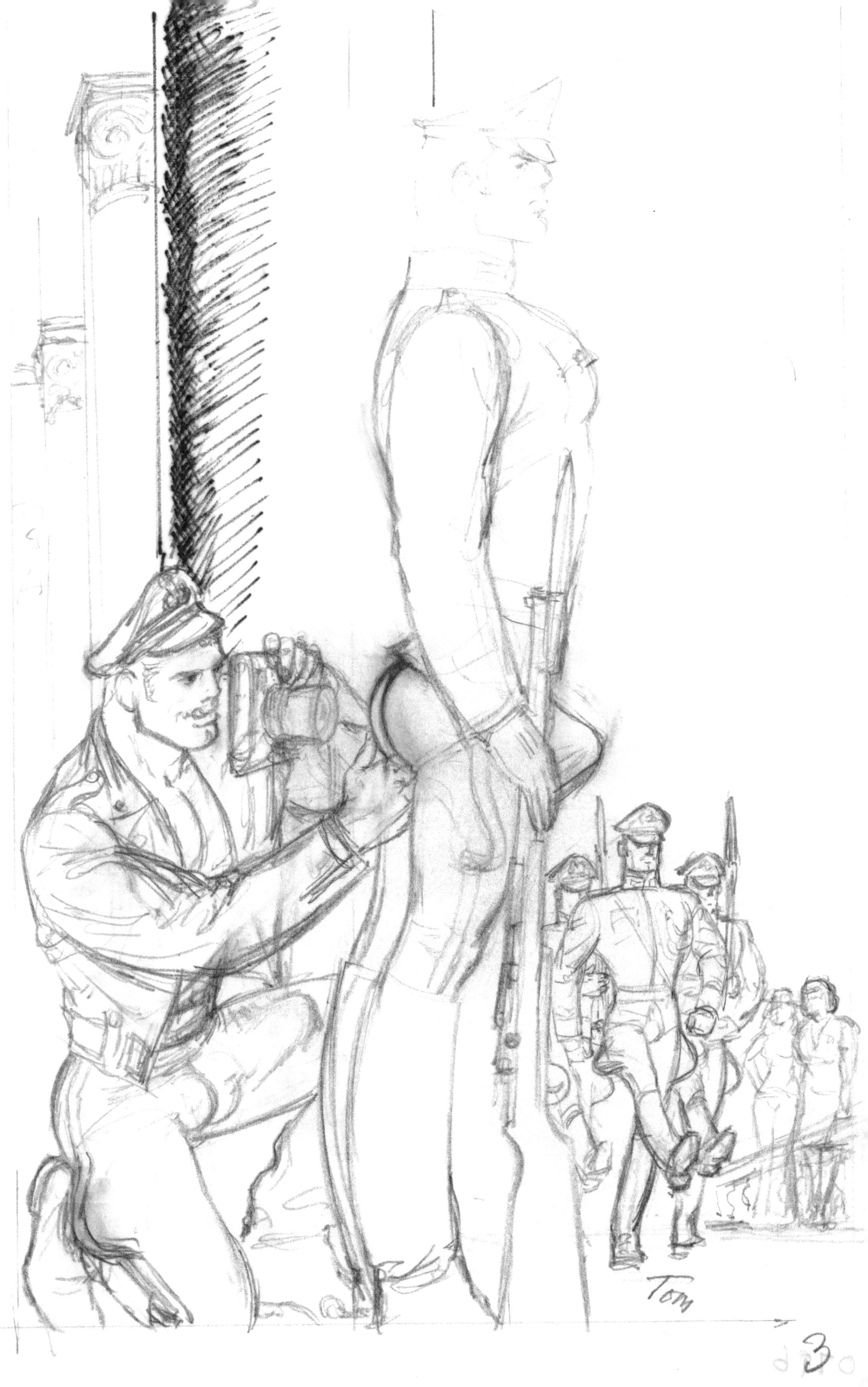Tom
3

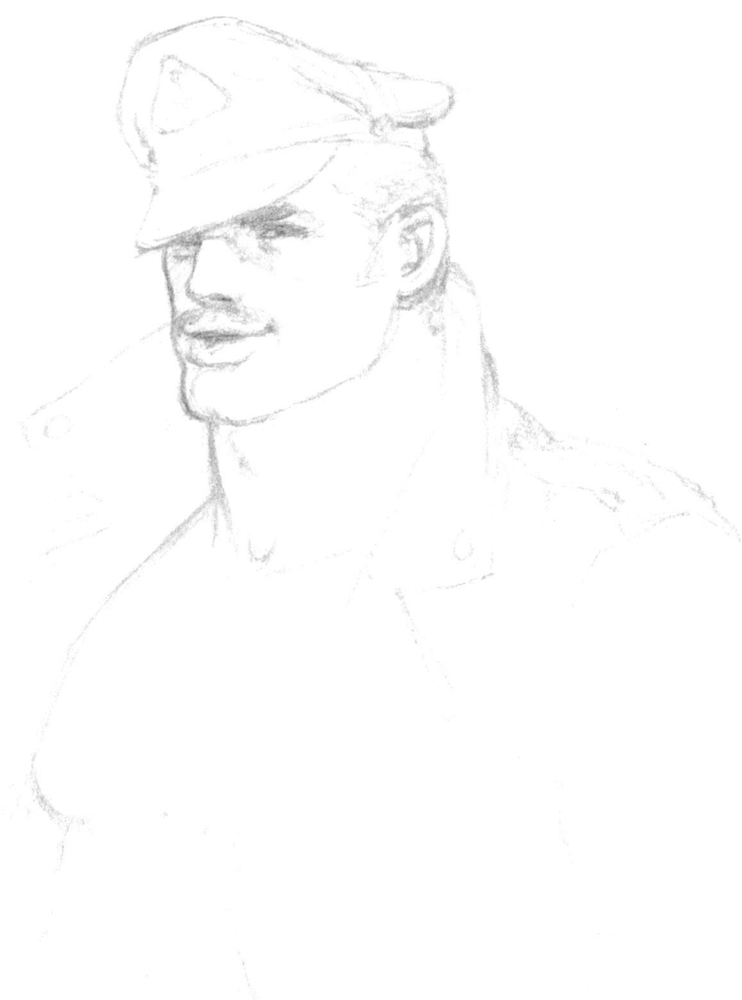

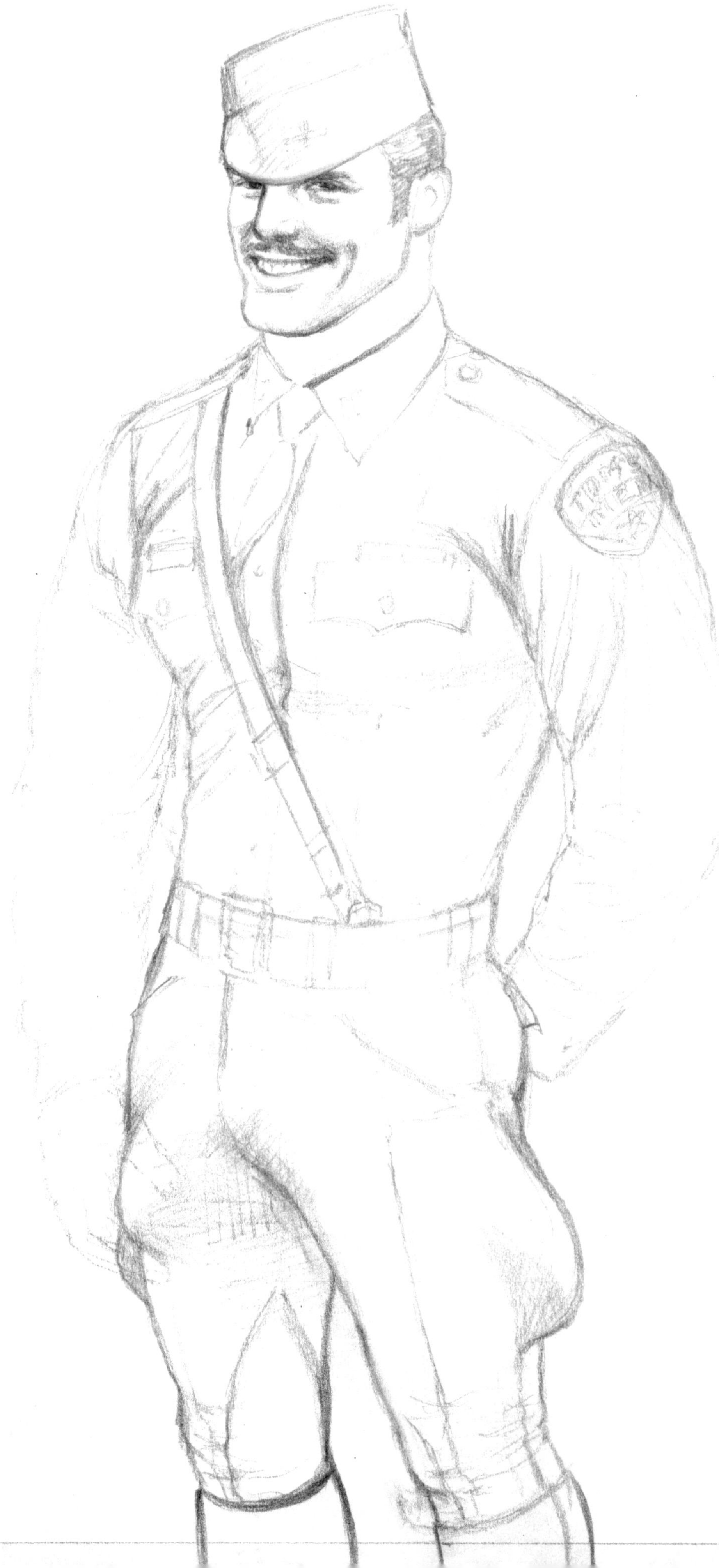

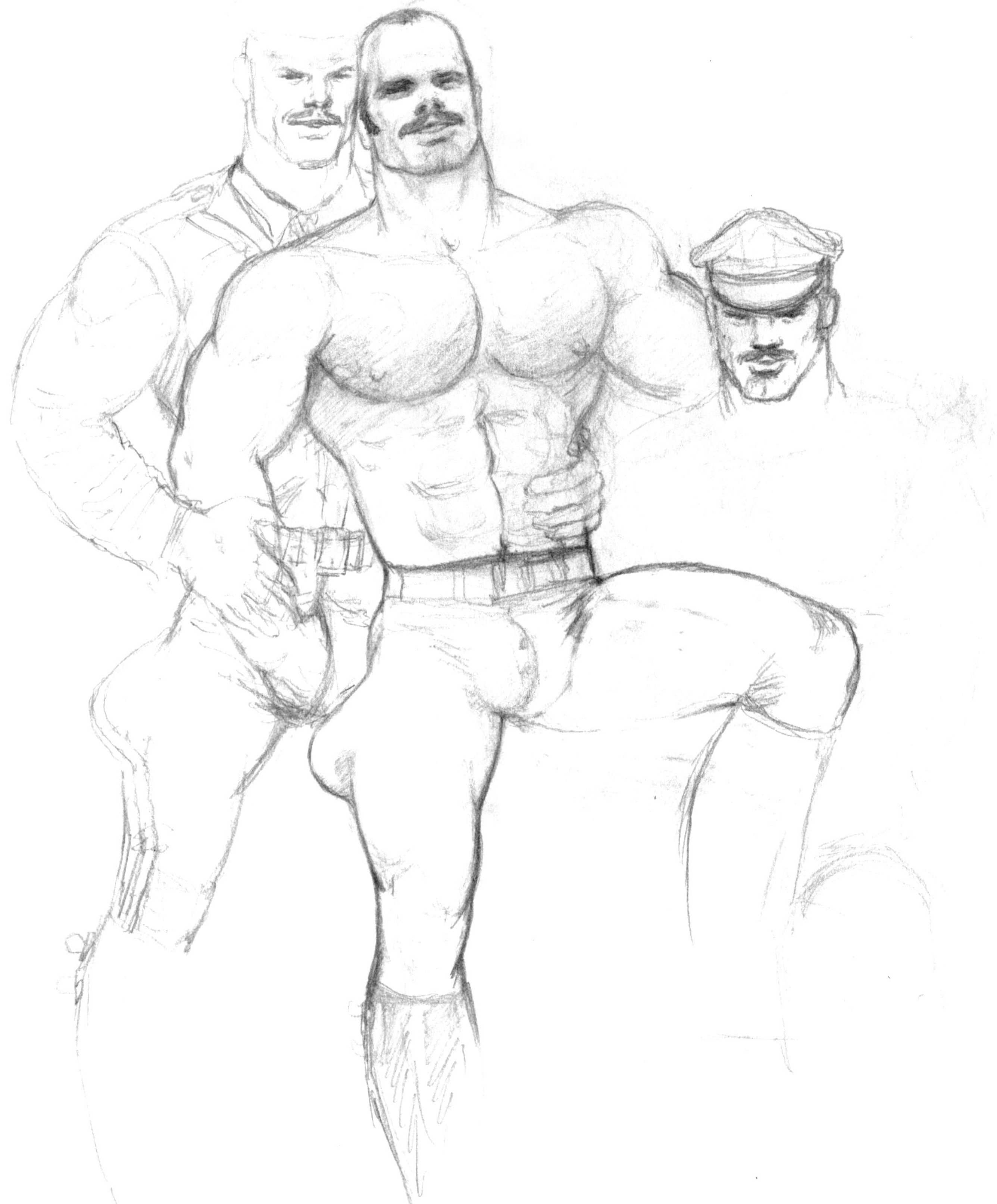

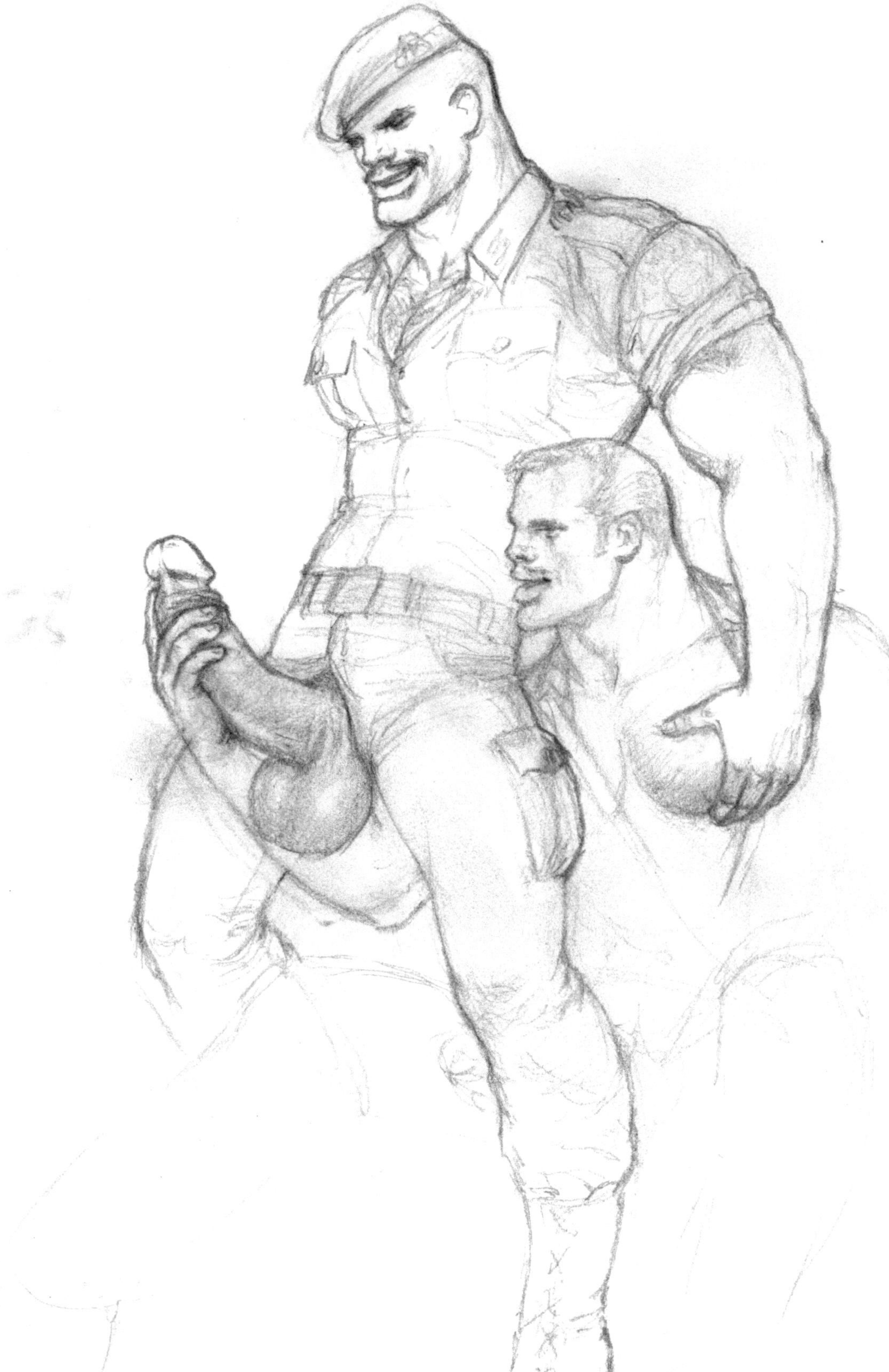

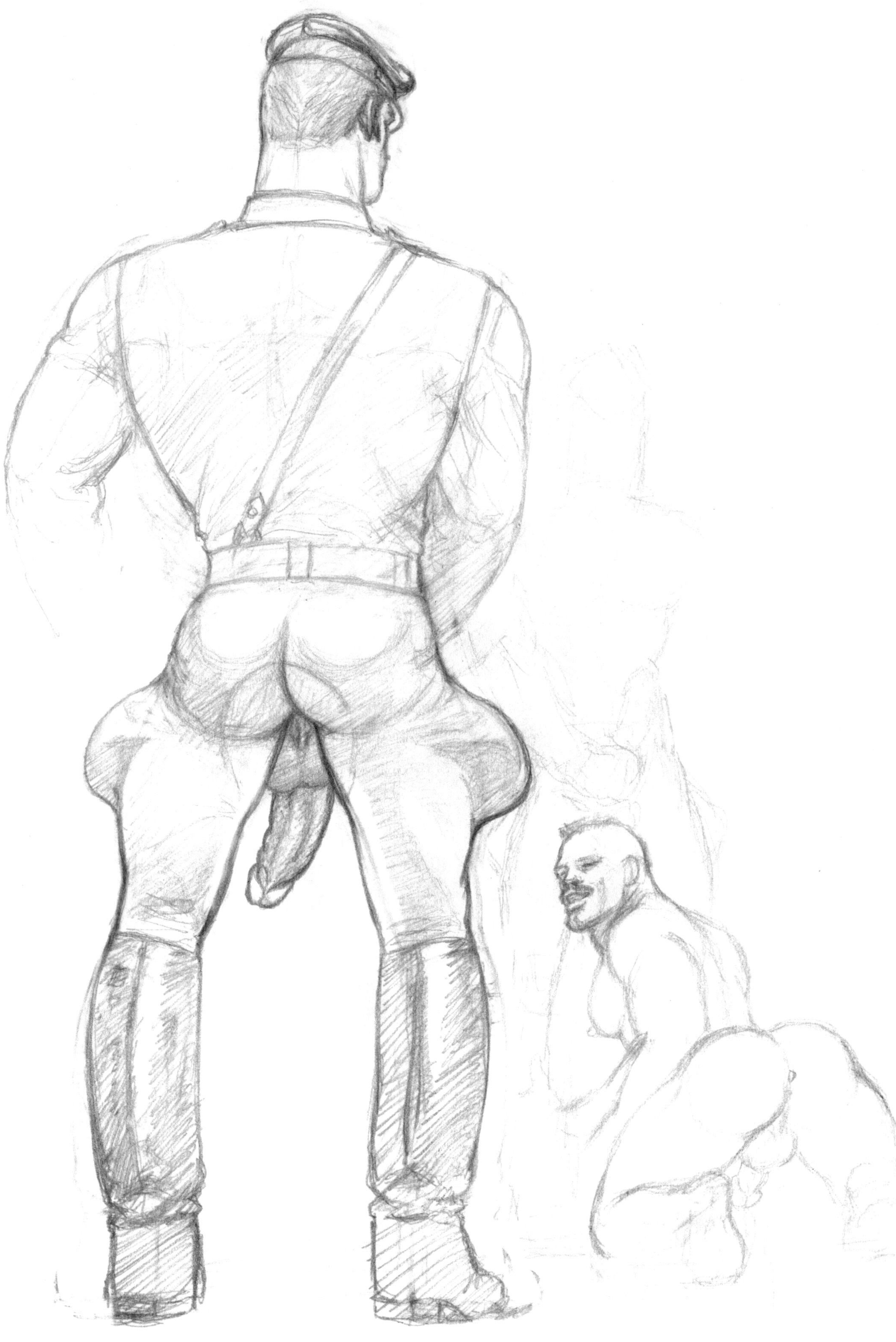

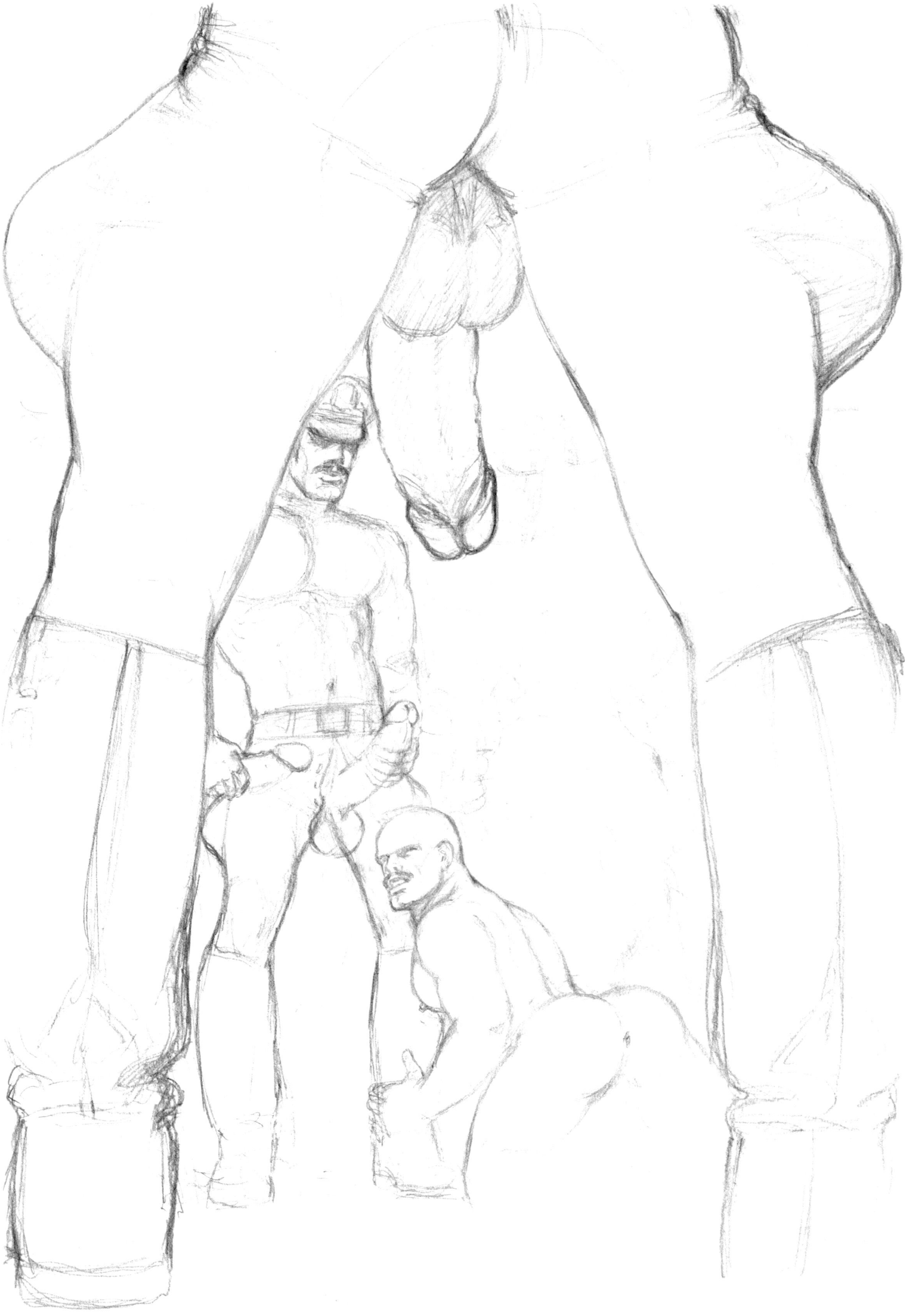

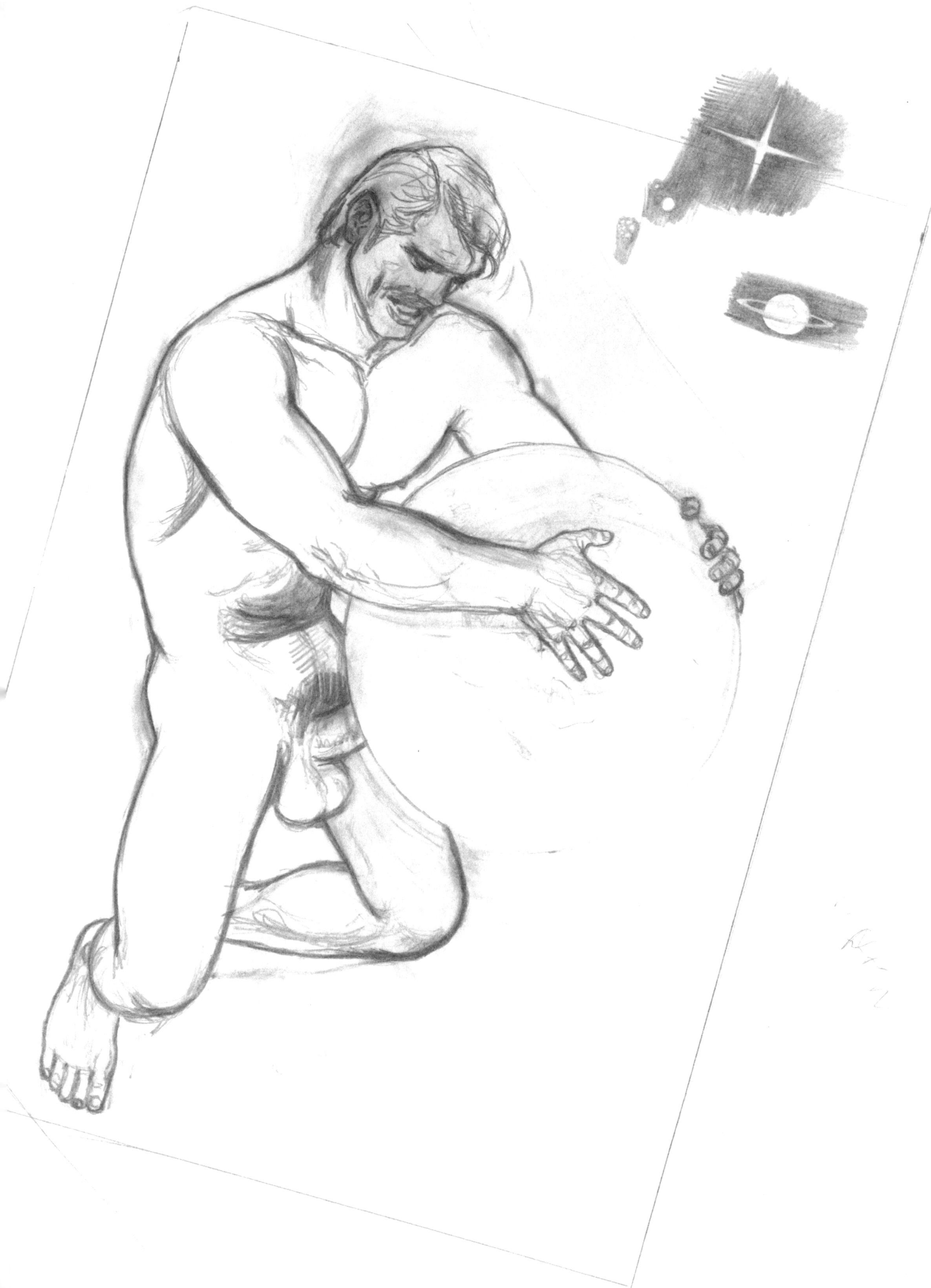

DRAWING IS PUTTING A LINE AROUND DESIRE

We are attracted to drawings, and particularly sketches, because their modesty of means and their unfinishedness allow an unobstructed insight into an artist's intention and vision. What we find in them is spontaneity, immediacy, bareness, subconsciousness and humor. Drawings are an artist's instant declaration of what is important and what is not. Sometimes their discontinuity and fragmentation confuse us. Their personal and often uninhibited content might make us feel uncomfortable. Yet the vigor, creative speculation and artistic freedom they offer will nevertheless draw us in. No pun intended. All of this holds true for the drawings of Tom of Finland (born Touko Laaksonen).

If we can agree upon the definition that great artists must be radical in the terms of their own time and have the power to change the way we see the world, then Tom of Finland undoubtedly counts among the great and truly influential artists of the late 20th century. He managed to gain a huge international following outside the usual precincts of museums and galleries. Through his iconic images, he almost single-handedly changed the way gay men were perceived by society, and – maybe even more important – how gay men perceived themselves. The massive oeuvre that he produced over the course of a career spanning nearly six decades is devoted almost entirely to this one topic – men, their bodies and their spirits. This extraordinary consistency in subject-matter was matched by a life-long passion for the supreme discipline of free-hand drawing. All he needed to create a universe of dazzlingly gorgeous hunks was a pencil and a sheet of paper. And he most likely drew every day of his life. Drawing, it seems, was an exercise for his restless imagination and desire.

Tom's world was populated by cowboys, mechanics, cops, punks and thugs – all indulging their desires with great camaraderie and without guilt or prejudice. This book assembles a cross-section of these characters as dreamt up by Tom in rough sketches or more carefully executed studies. Mostly they served as preliminary drawings for the highly finished works, many of which were intended for publication and thus a wide audience. The format of a sketchbook lets the viewer take an intimate glance over the artist's shoulder and share in his exuberant joie de vivre. It is not a facsimile of an actual sketchbook used by Tom of Finland, although we have sought to be as faithful to the originals as technically possible. Instead, the playful appearance of this book reflects the joy that Tom's art has brought us over the years.

All drawings in this book were on view in the first Tom of Finland exhibition at Galerie Judin in 2017 as loans from the Tom of Finland Foundation and we are deeply grateful to its president Durk Dehner, who in 1984 established the Foundation with Tom, and his partner and vice president S. R. Sharp for their ongoing support and trust.

Juerg Judin and Pay Matthis Karstens

Editors
Juerg Judin
Pay Matthis Karstens

Graphic design
Jakob Straub

Production
DruckConcept, Berlin

All works reproduced in this publication are from
Tom of Finland Foundation and used with their permission.

First published in Berlin in 2017 by Edition Judin.

This edition is published in Italy in 2022 by Skira editore S.p.A.
Palazzo Casati Stampa
Via Torino 61
20123 Milano Italy
www.skira.net

Paper
Lessebo Rough Ivory 150 g/m²
Les Naturales Azobébraun 630 g/m²

ISBN
978-88-572-4651-2

Distributed in USA, Canada, Central & South America by
ARTBOOK | D.A.P. 75 Broad Street Suite 630, New York, NY 10004, USA.
Distributed elsewhere in the world by
Thames and Hudson Ltd., 181A High Holborn, London WC1V 7QX, United Kingdom.

Printed and bound by
Printer Trento
Via alle Ròste, 12
38100 Trento, Italy

Tom of Finland
FOUNDATION